Guide for Weekend Prospectors

Easy Tests for Rocks and Minerals

by S. F. Wayland

hancock

house

ISBN 0-88839-405-5
Copyright © 1997 S. F. (Sidney Frank) Wayland

Cataloging in Publication Data

Wayland, S. F. (Sidney Frank), 1930-
   Identifying tests for weekend prospectors

ISBN 0-88839-405-5

1. Rocks–Identification–Popular works. 2. Mineralogy, Determinative–Popular works. 3. Prospecting–Popular works. I. Title
QE365.W39 1997   549.'1   C97-910096-8

Printed in Hong Kong—Colorcraft

Editor: Nancy Miller
Production: Sharon Boglari
Cover design: Andrew Jaster

Published simultaneously in Canada and the United States by

HANCOCK HOUSE PUBLISHERS LTD.
19313 Zero Avenue, Surrey, BC V4P 1M7
(604) 538-1114 Fax (604) 538-2262

HANCOCK HOUSE PUBLISHERS
1431 Harrison Avenue, Blaine, WA 98230-5005
(604) 538-1114 Fax (604) 538-2262

Contents

Dedication

To my wife June, my sister Iris, and to the memory of my mother.

Introduction

When (more years ago than I care to recall) I chose to rely less on other persons helping me to identify the minerals I had found, I realized I had a tough job ahead of me. To ease the task I decided to learn the ages-old arts of blowpiping, bead testing, flame testing and other such classification experiments. I read all the books I could find on the subject and after trying out some of the tests, found them to be much more fascinating and less arduous than first imagined. After I became comparatively proficient, I was brave (foolish?) enough to sit in at gem and mineral shows attempting to identify jewelry, or whatever the paying public placed before me; I also gave demonstrations of mineral testing. From there I progressed to imparting my self-taught knowledge to prospectors. Prompted by a request from a part-time prospector, I decided to put together this little book. Some parts of this book were formerly published in the magazine, *Canadian Rockhound*, sadly, no longer with us; for which, over a period of eight years, I was a contributor.

I hope this guide persuades people to go out and study the beauty this world has to offer, whether rocks and minerals, plants, birds or insects.

How to Use This Book

One of the primary uses of this book is to solve identification problems. As the book will likely be picked up and read from any specific point, rather than from beginning to end, I have tried to break the book up into a few separate sections (glossary, minerals, tests, etc.) with cross-references throughout. There is a glossary at the beginning of the book to help the rookie prospector who may be confused by terms not usually found in the common vocabulary. Following the glossary is a section which looks at more than twenty mineral elements, describing their visible properties, elemental makeup and tests with which to identify them. Where possible I have tried to describe the areas where the rocks are found. Unfortunately, there are very few hard and fast rules when it comes to locating certain specimens; and even when there are rules, the rocks don't always know them. The minerals and elements are cross-referenced with the appropriate identifying tests and equipment from the testing section. They aren't in alphabetical order, rather they are listed under their elemental names in a sequence which, in my estimation, rates their importance and the level of interest which surrounds them. However, in two instances, purely for clarity, I've listed the minerals under their common names because who, but a few, would look for diamond under carbon or for corundum (ruby, sapphire, etc.) under aluminum. They are followed by a chapter on rocks and minerals used in lapidary (meaning those specimens that, while not necessarily valuable, come to mind when one thinks of common gemstones that are made into ornaments).

The next section describes the making, or gathering together, of equipment needed to examine the assorted minerals, as well as the numerous tests that can be done to identify specimens. Most of the tests are relatively easy for beginners to perform, however some do require equipment, much of which is easy to make. (They, too, are cross-referenced by page number with the various minerals to which they pertain.) Within the section is a chapter which deals with examining minerals on a field trip, when one is limited as to what can be carried, to discover if they are worth further testing.

And finally, there is a field-testing index which goes over the sundry elements that can be tested while on a field trip, followed by an index listing rocks and minerals used in lapidary, and a general index.

It's then just a matter of practice, practice, practice.

Glossary

ADAMANTINE LUSTER: a very high luster that gives the appearance of being very hard—like a diamond.

AMPHIBOLE: the amphiboles are a large group of minerals having water as part of their composition. They are a parallel group to the pyroxenes. The member that attracts most of the attention is nephrite jade.

AQUA REGIA: "royal water," so named because it will dissolve "noble" elements—gold, platinum.

ARSENIDE: a mineral containing the element arsenic.

ARSENOPYRITE: a pathfinder iron mineral of little value, but sometimes found associated with gold not visible to the naked eye (invisible gold). Can be detected using *aqua regia* and metallic tin.

ASSAY: a particle or a fragment that is being testing.

BISMUTHINITE: a bismuth sulfide mined for the bismuth.

BLOWPIPING: a method of using a blowpipe, in conjunction with a candle flame or alcohol lamp flame, to identify a mineral specimen on a charcoal block, or plaster of Paris block, or with platinum wire and a flux.

BORATE: a mineral formed by the chemical action of boric acid and an element.

BORAX BEAD: a globule formed in the loop at the end of a piece of platinum wire which had previously been dipped into borax powder. The bead is formed by heat from a blowpipe and candle flame or alcohol lamp flame. See p.74, 76.

BORNITE: a common copper sulfide mineral.

CARBONADO: a diamond; grayish black to black, is opaque and without cleavage, unlike most diamonds. I believe it is the toughest, hardest substance known.

CARBONATE: a mineral formed by the chemical action of carbonic acid and an element; neutralizing the acid.

CARBON DIOXIDE: CO_2, the gas given off when carbonates come in contact with some acids.

CHALCEDONY: is a variety of quartz, usually transparent or translucent, jewelry, etc. Remember, chalcedony is pronounced as if the **ch** is a **k**.

CHALCANTHITE: another word where the **ch** is pronounced as a **k**. It is a naturally formed copper sulfate, quite poisonous.

CHERT: like chalcedony, it is a variety of quartz, usually opaque, with the impurities providing a wide range of colors. Another favorite of rockhounds.

CLEAVAGE: is the propensity for some minerals to break along well-defined lines, fluorite is a very good example. Some cleavage crystals give the appearance of a cut gem stones.

DECOMPOSE: minerals are said to decompose when they separate into the constituent elements. In chalcopyrite the copper and sulfur separate and depart, leaving the iron to rust.

EARTHY LUSTER: roughly speaking, the gloss or sheen of dry soil.

EFFERVESCENCE: the giving off of bubbles of gas as the result of chemical action.

ELEMENT: any of more than 100 different, inseparable substances, which together, or alone, act as the building blocks of all matter—gold, carbon, sodium, lead, aluminum, calcium and so forth. Sorted into certain families sharing characteristics on the periodic table of elements.

EVOLUTION: in mineral testing, usually the giving off of a gas.

FLUORESCENCE: some minerals, when subjected to ultraviolet light, absorb the light invisible to us and then emit longer light waves we can see; often turning dull specimens into objects of pure beauty. The name comes from the mineral fluorite.

FLUX: a substance, or mixture, employed to aid fusion of metals and minerals.

FRACTURE: is almost the direct opposite of cleavage in a mineral. Whereas the latter produces mostly smooth, flat faces, fractures are usually rough and misshapen. Conchoidal fractures (see left) are the possible exception, with shell-like scoops pleasing to the eye. This way of fracturing allowed early man to produce tools and weapons with cherts, obsidian, etc.

Conchoidal fractures allowed early man to fashion tools similar to the one illustrated.

GANGUE: a general term for minerals and rocks of no value, found with desirable, economic minerals.

GLASSY LUSTER: similar to the appearance of ordinary, clear window glass.

GOETHITE: an iron mineral, only important when found in huge amounts; an oxide.

GOSSAN OR IRON HAT: an area of rock, or soil and rocks, covered with a fairly heavy, yellowish brown coating of iron oxide. This usually occurs when a mineral containing iron is subjected to weathering, leaving behind the iron in the form of rust.

GREASE FITTING: if you have a vehicle, you have from 8 to 12 grease fittings in various parts of the steering mechanism. Grease is pumped through them to lubricate the moving parts. I found a grease fitting to be almost the perfect end for a blowpipe.

GREASY LUSTER: having the appearance of a greasy shine.

HALIDE: a mineral having a mixture of a halogen and a metal. Halogens are a group of elements on the periodic table that include iodine, chlorine, fluorine and bromine. Salt is a halide, being a compound of a metal (sodium) and a halogen (chlorine).

HEFT: the heaviness of an object. In the field, judged by weighing in the hand. See specific gravity.

HEXAGONITE: along with tremolite and nephrite jade, it is an amphibole mineral.

HIDDENITE: a gem variety of the mineral spodumene. Can be considered a source of lithium. The only difference between hiddenite and kunzite is color. Hiddenite has some shade of green; kunzite has some shade of violet.

INCLUSIONS: inclusions, for the purpose of this book, are best described as foreign bodies within transparent or translucent specimens. I liken them to imitation flowers, imitation pearls, beads, etc., found in glass paperweights.

INFUSIBLE: a term given to minerals that won't melt in a blowpipe flame, even on the thinnest edges, i.e., corundum.

IRIDESCENCE: showing the colors similar to the rainbow; often changing as an object is moved, i.e., chalcopyrite.

KUNZITE: another gem variety of the mineral spodumene, a source of lithium that is slightly violet in color.

LUSTER: the shine, or lack of it, of a specimen held in the hand, produced by reflected light.

METALLIC LUSTER: shining like a metal, i.e., pyrite, galena, chalcopyrite, etc.

MINERAL: is a natural substance not organic—animal or vegetable—with a definite chemical composition, found in the earth. A mineral is made up of elements.

MOHS' SCALE: A scale of hardness in which a mineral of a higher number can scratch all those below it, enabling the hardness of a mineral to be roughly calculated. If a mineral can be scratched by corundum but will scratch quartz, it could be topaz or another mineral with a hardness of 8. The names of the ten minerals are easily recalled, by saying the sentence: **The Girls Can Flirt And Other Quaint Things Can Do.**
1—Talc; 2—Gypsum; 3—Calcite; 4—Fluorite; 5—Apatite; 6—Orthoclase; 7—Quartz; 8—Topaz; 9—Corundum; 10—Diamond

MURATIC ACID: impure hydrochloric acid, but can be used in place of it. Besides, it's much cheaper.

NATIVE ELEMENTS: elements occurring naturally in an almost pure state, i.e., gold, sulfur, bismuth, copper, etc.

NICHROME: a trademark name for an alloy containing 60 percent nickel, 24 percent iron, 16 percent chrome, and a trace of carbon. Nichrome wire is a good substitute for platinum wire, and a lot cheaper. It can be used for bead testing cobalt and manganese because they both produce strong colors. However, it is not advisable for testing minerals with weaker colors, since the nickel, iron or chrome in the wire, could add their own colors to the bead.

NITRATE: a mineral formed chemically by the action of nitric acid and an element, with the acid becoming neutralized in the process. Nitrates are employed in fertilizers and explosives.

OCTAHEDRON: an eight-sided figure resembling two pyramids glued base to base.

OPAQUE: as the dictionary says, not transparent or translucent. In other words, a specimen that won't let light through except at very thin edges.

ORTHOCLASE FELDSPAR: a fairly common mineral of little value, easy to identify—see Field Tests. At 6 on Mohs' scale of hardness. Pink specimens have been mistaken for pale rhodonite. Often forms the crystals known as phenocrysts in porphyry.

OXIDE: a mineral with oxygen as part of the compound. Some are very hard, such as corundum and cassiterite.

PATHFINDER MINERAL: a mineral of little value economically but which could possibly lead to the finding of a mineral of importance.

PEARLY LUSTER: a sheen similar to that of a pearl, or the inside surface of some bivalve sea shells.

PENTLANDITE: an iron-nickel sulfide, important for the nickel.

PHOSPHATE: a mineral formed when phosphoric acid comes in contact with an element and in the process neutralizes the acid.

PHOSPHORESCENCE: the light emitted from a mineral that continues after the cause of the glow has been taken away. Comparable to the glow from the hands and numbers of a luminous watch, when the light activating it has been removed. Similar thermoluminescence is caused by heat.

PIPE COUPLING: a short piece of pipe with female threads (internal threads) in both ends, used for joining two pieces of pipe with male threads (external threads).

PITCHLIKE LUSTER: a sheen similar to the appearance of tar used on the roads when comparatively fresh.

PRECIPITATE: an easily seen substance produced by chemical action, often in a test tube, when two different chemical compounds, at least one a liquid, are brought together.

PROUSTITE: a common silver sulfide mineral.

PYRARGYRITE: a common silver sulfide mineral.

PYROXENE: the pyroxenes are a group of water-free silicates, including jadeite, rhodonite, spodumene.

PYRRHOTITE: a pathfinder mineral, an iron of little value that is sometimes found associated with nickel. In other words, first locate the pyrrhotite and it could lead to the nickel.

RESINOUS LUSTER: a yellowish luster somewhat like the resin exuded by pine trees and other conifers.

RETORT: a partially sealed container that prevents oxygen from entering during dry distillation.

SECONDARY MINERALS: when primary minerals, such as galena, pyrite, chalcopyrite and sphalerite, located in the upper parts of mineral veins, are subjected to oxidizing waters descending through them, the liquids often carry away some of the elements to form secondary minerals beneath, sometimes with oxygen as part of the new compounds.

SECTILE: a mineral is said to be sectile when it can be cut with a knife without powdering.

SILICATES: a complex group containing roughly half of the known minerals and, generally, the most difficult to identify with the usual tests. They are most often light in weight, quite hard and translucent, so they provide good lapidary materials. They are compounds of silicic acid and metals.

SILKY LUSTER: fibrous, somewhat like the luster from strands of silk.

SKUTTERUDITE: a cobalt-nickel-iron arsenide, mined mainly for the cobalt.

SPECIFIC GRAVITY: also known as relative density, with water given the value of 1, is best described as the weight of a mineral specimen when compared with the weight of an equal volume of water. Here are a few of the specific gravities of some minerals and a native element.

Serpentine—2.5; Topaz—3.5; Cassiterite—7.0; Cinnabar—8.0; Gold—19.3

Which means, if a cup of water weighs in at 1 pound, and if it was possible to fill a cup of similar size solidly with pure gold, the latter would weigh just more than 19 pounds.

SPINEL: an oxide; is hard at 8 on Mohs' scale, can be found in most colors. Can be mistaken for other jewels, especially ruby. The Black Prince's ruby in the British crown jewels, once thought to be a ruby, is a spinel.

STIBNITE: an antimony sulfide.

STREAK: the powder of a mineral obtained when a specimen is rubbed across a streak plate.

SUBLIMATE: in a closed tube, a sublimate is a deposit on the inside of the test tube, usually above and apart from the fragment being heated. In the case of opal, the identifying sublimate would be colorless drops of water. See closed tube testing illustration in section on Opal on p.46.

SUBMETALLIC LUSTER: a sheen less than metallic, except when enhanced by a bright light or when it is wet.

SULFATE: a mineral formed by the chemical action of sulfuric acid and a metal. The process is easily copied by dropping a piece of copper into sulfuric acid, with copper sulfate resulting.

SULFIDE: a mineral with sulfur (not sulfuric acid) as part of the mix such as galena and chalcopyrite.

TARNISH: a metallic mineral is said to be tarnished when the color of the surface differs from that of a freshly fractured surface, i.e., bornite and chalcopyrite.

THERMOLUMINESCENCE: the glowing from a fragment of a mineral, after being held, briefly, in the side of a candle or alcohol lamp flame and then being removed. Best seen in a darkened room. Try fluorite.

TRANSLUCENT: a material is said to be translucent when it allows light waves to pass through, but is not clear enough for objects to be seen through it.

TRANSPARENT: an object is transparent when it allows light waves to pass through and is clear enough for objects to be seen through it.

TREMOLITE: the white member of the group of minerals that includes nephrite jade.

TRIBOLUMINESCENT: minerals said to be so, give off visible light when mechanical force (sawing, scratching, hitting with a hammer) is applied.

TUNGSTATE: a mineral formed by the chemical action of tungstic acid and an element.

VITREOUS LUSTER: I like to think of it as just below the brilliance of adamantine but above glassy. This luster is similar to that of the edge of a freshly broken piece of window glass appearing brighter than the glass surface.

WEATHERING: the actions of rain, wind, frost, snow, etc., in breaking up and altering rocks and minerals.

WILLEMITE: a zinc silicate mined for the metallic element.

WOLFRAMITE: a tungstate of iron and manganese mined for the tungsten.

Minerals and Native Elements

Diamonds

Prior to the discovery of diamonds in northern Canada, they had been found in North America, principally in the U.S. and particularly in Arkansas. Those found scattered about in the eastern states are thought, by some, to have originated in Canada and been deposited there by glaciers. Their main uses are as abrasives, because of their hardness, and in jewelry.

Visible properties: Diamonds range from colorless through shades of yellow, orange, red, green, blue, brown to black. *Luster:* adamantine; most often transparent to translucent and opaque. *Hardness:* as mentioned, diamonds are one of the minerals in Mohs' scale of hardness, at 10. Some varieties cleave or fracture easily; except carbonado, one of the toughest minerals known.

Makeup: pure carbon (C).

Tests:

1. The best test to quickly identify a diamond from other glassy minerals (quartz, corundum, etc.) in the field, is to carry a piece of tungsten-carbide (one of the hardest man-made alloys, and obtainable in even the smallest of communities from machine shops). Only a diamond, of all natural substances, is hard enough to easily scratch tungsten-carbide. The mark is then checked under magnification to ensure it is a scratch, and not a streak left on the testing surface by a softer mineral. Equipment needed: a piece of tungsten-carbide.
2. If, when subjected to short-wave ultraviolet light, the specimen fluoresces it can be a diamond. Equipment needed: a short-wave UV light.
3. Others emit visible light (known as triboluminescence) when subjected to stroking (scratching) with a metal point. These flashes of

light are best seen in a darkened room. Caution: gem stones could be harmed by some of these testing methods; so the best determining test is to compare the brilliant, hard luster with other less-brilliant gem stones (white sapphire, spinel, etc.). Equipment needed: a pointed metal rod.

Comments:

The above tests help a person decide if a specimen is, in fact, a diamond, not quartz, corundum or other glassy minerals. The first test should be all that is necessary.

Graphite, also pure carbon, is at the other end of the hardness scale and is one of the softest minerals. Diamonds can be reduced to graphite by intensely heating.

See: how to make a set of hardness points, p.59; also a description of Mohs' scale of hardness in relation to them, p.60.

Corundum

Corundum occurs in some parts of North America, including Canada. In fact, a large deposit was recently found in Labrador. At one time it was used as an abrasive until largely superseded by man-made materials (carborundum). It is also used in jewelry.

Visible properties: It can be found from transparent to translucent: *colors* range from clear to white, yellow, gray, blue, red, violet, brown and black. *Hardness:* 9, one of the minerals in Mohs' scale of hardness. *Luster*: vitreous to adamantine.

Makeup: aluminum (Al) + oxygen (O).

Tests:

1. Only diamond is harder among natural minerals, corundum will scratch topaz. Equipment needed: a piece of topaz. If this test is positive, go to the fifth test for further verification.
2. It often fluoresces under short-wave ultraviolet light. Equipment needed: a short-wave UV lamp.
3. Corundum is insoluble (won't dissolve) in acids. Equipment needed: a test tube, nitric acid, an alcohol lamp.
4. Is infusible (won't melt) on charcoal. Equipment needed: a charcoal block, a blowpipe, alcohol lamp.

5. Finely powdered corundum strongly heated on a charcoal block with a blowpipe and alcohol lamp will, upon the application of cobalt nitrate and reheating, give a beautiful blue color indicating aluminum. Like diamond, corundum is often triboluminescent. Equipment needed: a charcoal block, a blowpipe, an alcohol lamp, cobalt nitrate.

Comments:

Clear varieties of this mineral supply us with the magnificent gem stones rubies and sapphires, the metal oxide impurities provide the different colors.

See: how to produce charcoal blocks, p.60; how to make a blowpipe, p.63; how to make an alcohol lamp, p.73; how to produce cobalt nitrate, p.78; diluting acids, p.81.

Gold

The most popular metal for jewelry, and the best for filling teeth, gold is found over much of North America. Its uses are numerous and varied. It is most often discovered by weekend prospectors, glistening in the bottom of a gold pan amid the black sand (magnetite).

Visible properties: A rich yellow color when pure, gold is less yellow when alloyed with silver (as it often is naturally). *Luster:* metallic. *Hardness:* 2.5 to 3. *Heaviness:* varying from 15.5 to 19.3 specific gravity, depending on silver content. Native gold gives a gold streak on a streak plate, unlike other goldlike minerals, such as pyrite and chalcopyrite, that give greenish black to black streaks.

Makeup: gold (Au), but often associated with silver (Ag); sometimes copper (Cu) and iron (Fe).

Tests:

1. A rock that appears to contain minute particles of gold (but which could be yellow mica, pyrite or chalcopyrite) should be broken into small pieces, the pieces crushed to powder and panned. Any gold will be found in the bottom of the pan long after the gangue is gone.
2. A rock that is thought to contain gold but has no sparkling yellows as visible clues, should be crushed to a powder and boiled with *aqua regia* in a test tube over an alcohol lamp until enough of the mineral has dissolved. If gold is present, the addition of metallic tin will turn

the solution a purple color (purple of Cassius).

3. On a charcoal block heated by a blowpipe and alcohol lamp, a tiny piece of gold-bearing rock will release the precious metal into a yellow button, readily flattened with a hammer without shattering.

4. An unstamped gold ring, bracelet, etc., (or one in which the hallmark has worn away) can be proven to be gold, if a clean portion of the metal is brought in contact with a clean droplet of mercury, and the mercury adheres to and coats the gold. The mercury coating is then removed with an application of iodine.

See: how to use a streak plate and alternatives, p.79; how to make a small crusher, p.80; how to produce *aqua regia*, p.80; how to use a blowpipe and alcohol lamp, p.73; sources of mercury, p.81.

Silver

Although native silver isn't a particularly rare element, argentite is the most common silver mineral mined in Canada, followed by pyrargyrite and proustite. Silver is often found with lead, particularly with the lead mineral galena. Like gold, silver is used in many different ways such as in jewelry, in photography, and for plating cutlery and trays.

Visible properties: Argentite is easily cut with a knife (sectile); the others are brittle. Proustite is usually some shade of brilliant red; pyrargyrite is a deep red to black; and argentite is dark gray to blackish. *Hardness*: all range from 2 to 2.5. *Luster:* argentite is metallic; pyrargyrite ranges from metallic to adamantine; proustite is adamantine. In the same order the first has a shiny *streak* dark gray to black; the second red to purplish; the last some shade of brilliant red.

Makeup: the element silver (Ag) is mostly found in association with other elements such as sulfur (S), the combination of the two elements in different ratios results in different silver minerals. When the elements silver and sulphur are combined with the element arsenic (As) the resulting chemical composition is that of the silver mineral called proustite; when combined with antimony (Sb) the silver mineral pyrargyrite is the result.

Tests:

1. Crush to a powder a small portion of the possible silver mineral, mix with either baking or washing soda, place in the small depression in a charcoal block, heat strongly in the reducing flame with a blowpipe

and alcohol lamp and, if silver is present, a bright, white globule of the desired metal is produced; it will flatten with several blows from a hammer. Equipment needed: a rock crusher, a charcoal block, an alcohol lamp, a blowpipe and a hammer.

2. To double check: drop the flattened mass into a test tube with dilute nitric acid and boil over the alcohol lamp until dissolved. Upon the addition of dilute hydrochloric acid (or a few grains of salt) a white precipitate should form. If the precipitate is curdlike much silver is present; getting milkier with lesser amounts. If left exposed to bright light for several hours, the contents of the test tube darken considerably (hence its use in photography). Equipment needed: nitric acid (dilute), an alcohol lamp, hydrochloric acid (dilute) or salt, a test tube.

3. To prove whether an ashtray, a piece of cutlery or jewelry, etc., is made of silver, simply smear on the clean metal surface a portion of the liquid yolk from a fried or boiled egg. If the object is silver, and after the sulfur in the yolk has had time to do the job, a dark stain should be seen when the dried yolk is removed. Other sulfur compounds also give similar, but quicker, results. A small piece of an iron pill, ferrous sulfate (often taken by anemic persons and sold in drugstores), or granular moss killer (a mixture of sulfates), when combined with soda and charcoal dust, moistened, and heated in the cavity in a charcoal block with a blowpipe and alcohol lamp in the reducing flame, is usable similar to egg yolk; except a few drops of water are added to the fused mass after placing on the object being tested. Again the blackish stain indicates silver. Equipment needed: a fried or boiled egg or an iron pill, baking or washing soda, charcoal dust, a charcoal block, a blowpipe and an alcohol lamp.

4. However, these results can also occur with a silver-plated object; so, to differentiate between solid silver and silver plate (usually plated over a copper alloy) make a tiny scratch on the object, where it won't be seen, and apply a drop of dilute nitric acid. In a few minutes, if plated over a copper alloy, the acid drop starts to turn green; then upon the addition of dilute ammonia, it turns a beautiful blue. If solid silver, there's no reaction to unheated dilute nitric acid. This test can also be employed on gold objects to discover whether they're solid gold or plated. Equipment needed: nitric acid (dilute), ammonia.

Comments:

A professor of geology whom I heard lecture a number of times, mentioned a successful prospecting trip he'd undertaken to a scrap-metal yard. While browsing, he came across some unusual-looking metal bars.

He asked the person in charge of the yard the price for the bars and, because they'd been around a long time and the man wanted to be rid of them, he got them for next to nothing. You guessed it—they were solid silver.

See: diluting acids, p.81; how to use a streak plate, p.79; how to make a small rock crusher, p.80; how to make an alcohol lamp, p.73; how to make a blowpipe, p.63.

Copper

Copper was known and worked by North American Indians long before Europeans arrived. They procured it from outcroppings. Today, although copper in its elemental state is still mined, chalcopyrite and bornite are more important mineral sources of the metal, because they are more common. There are many other minerals in which copper is part, in varying amounts, of the whole. There are producing copper mines in many parts of Canada, however some are closed down until the price of copper goes up. Copper is used for water pipes and other tubings, among other things, and when alloyed (mixed) with zinc it produces brass, with tin it makes bronze.

Visible properties: When freshly exposed, the mineral chalcopyrite is golden, but rapidly tarnishes and becomes iridescent. *Luster:* metallic. *Hardness:* 3.5 to 4, and easily scratched with a knife blade (unlike pyrite, which it closely resembles, with a hardness of 6 to 6.5, and is unscratchable with a knife). *Streak*: blackish.
Bornite, when freshly exposed, is bronzelike. *Luster:* metallic, it tarnishes to an attractive purple, readily, when opened to the elements—leading to the popular name, peacock ore. *Hardness:* 3, like chalcopyrite, it is brittle. *Streak*: light grayish black.

Makeup: both minerals are mixtures of copper (Cu) + iron (Fe) + sulfur (S). Bornite has the higher copper content.

Tests:

1. Most copper minerals identify themselves with a simple test. Crush a particle to powder, place it in the concave side of a watch glass or a lens removed from an old pair of spectacles, and add a few drops of dilute hydrochloric acid. Remove the paper from the end of a twist-tie, make a loop on the bared end, dip the loop into the mixture and place into the side of an alcohol (or candle) flame. After several times of dipping into the powder and acid, some of the solid gets burned onto the wire; then, if copper is present, a lovely blue will color the

side and top of the flame. Remember: never use an iron wire for more than a single test; platinum wire should never be employed to flame test possible copper minerals, because it's difficult to completely remove all of the copper. Equipment needed: a rock crusher, spectacle lens, hydrochloric acid (dilute), a twist tie, an alcohol lamp.

2. Another test (only mentioned here because it gives such a positive result) involves boiling the crushed particle in dilute nitric acid until a green solution forms (indicating copper), and when a few drops of ammonia are added to the solution it turns a beautiful blue, with the iron seen as a reddish brown precipitate. Equipment needed: nitric acid (dilute), an alcohol lamp, ammonia, a test tube.

Comments:

Due to weathering, a hidden copper deposit will sometimes reveal itself, to an observant prospector, by coloring the surrounding rock a pretty green known as copper stain.

The crystals of some copper minerals are much sought after by collectors, because of their wonderful colors.

See: flame tests, p.82; streak tests, p.79; diluting acids, p.81; how to make an alcohol lamp, p.73; how to make a rock crusher, p.80.

Lead

Galena, another sulfide (a compound with the element sulfur), is the principal ore (a natural mineral) of lead. It is mined in many regions of the world; is mentioned in the Old Testament; and was one of the first metals used by man. At one time there were many producing mines in the central Kootenay region of British Columbia. Lead is used in vehicle batteries, solders, soft hammers, fishing weights and used to be employed as roofing in old buildings.

Visible properties: *color* and *streak* are both pencil-lead gray. *Luster:* metallic. *Hardness:* 2.5 to 2.75.

Makeup: lead (Pb) + sulfur (S); often with one or more of the following: silver (Ag), gold (Au), antimony (Sb), zinc (Zn), selenium (Se), cadmium (Cd), bismuth (Bi), copper (Cu) and arsenic (As).

Tests:

1. Galena is often recognized by color and heft alone, as it has a fairly

high specific gravity of 7.6.

2. A good test to identify galena and other lead minerals, involves mixing 1 part charcoal dust, 1 part mineral and 3 parts soda, moistening, placing into the cavity in a charcoal block and, with a blowpipe and alcohol lamp, heating in the reducing flame. This, if lead is present, will produce tiny globules of the metal, a yellow coating nearby, and a white coating with a bluish border further away. The lead globules are easier to flatten than silver (mentioned earlier). Equipment needed: charcoal dust and a block, baking or washing soda, blowpipe, an alcohol lamp, a hammer and a rock crusher.

3. On a plaster of Paris block with iodide flux, the same heating procedure produces a chrome yellow coating. Equipment needed: a plaster of Paris block, iodide flux, a blowpipe, an alcohol lamp, a hammer and a rock crusher.

4. The test I prefer is to boil some of the powdered mineral in dilute hydrochloric acid in a test tube until dissolved (a rotten-egg smell indicates a sulfide). Upon the addition of a potassium iodide solution, if lead is present, a yellow precipitate is seen. Equipment needed: a test tube, hydrochloric acid (dilute), an alcohol lamp, potassium iodide solution and a rock crusher.

Comments:

Don't worry about burning one's self when heating a mineral fragment on a charcoal block. It won't catch fire. Also, at 1 inch x 1 inch x 4 inch long (25 mm x 25 mm x 100 mm long), the block keeps fingers well away from the heat.

The symbol for lead, Pb, comes from *plumbum*, Latin for the metal. The word plumber, meaning a worker in lead, comes from the same source. But today, few plumbers work with the metal, other than during soldering, that gave their trade its name.

See: how to make plaster of Paris blocks, p.63; chemicals, and how some are prepared, p.83; using a streak plate, p.79; how to make a blowpipe, p.63; how to make an alcohol lamp, p.73; diluting acids, p.81; how to make a rock crusher, p.80.

Iron

Iron has been employed by man for many centuries, in one way or another; especially when it was discovered that upon the addition of carbon, it became the much stronger and more flexible steel. It is a very common element found almost everywhere. Most larger countries have an abundance of it; and Canada has a fair share. Iron is used in steel alloys, as cast iron, and where its tendency to oxidize can be controlled.

Magnetite, as the name implies, is one iron mineral of only a few that will react to a magnet. Another iron mineral, pyrrhotite, also reacts, except the attraction can range from weak to strong. Limonite and goethite, although listed as separate minerals, can be lumped together, because it's sometimes difficult to determine where one ends and the other begins. Hematite is the most economically important iron mineral. It's also employed in lapidary (Alaska Black Diamond) and polishing (jeweler's rouge).

Visible properties: Magnetite is black and *streaks* black. *Luster:* metallic. *Hardness:* 6.

Pyrrhotite is a bronze color. *Luster:* metallic. *Streak:* grayish black. *Hardness:* 3.5 to 4.5.

Limonite and goethite range from yellow through brown to blackish brown in color. *Streak:* yellow, brownish yellow to brown. *Luster:* from dull and earthy to glassy, silky, submetallic and close to adamantine. *Hardness:* to 5.5.

Hematite is red (earthy), dark steel gray or black in color. *Streak:* some shade of light to dark red (hence being named after blood) or reddish brown. *Luster:* earthy and dull to metallic. *Hardness:* to 6.5.

Makeup: Magnetite—iron (Fe) + oxygen (O).

Pyrrhotite—iron (Fe) + sulfur (S); sometimes with nickel (Ni) and copper (Cu), when it's considered of enough importance to mine (see Nickel, p.25).

Limonite-Goethite—iron (Fe) + oxygen (O) + water (H_2O).

Hematite—iron (Fe) + oxygen (O).

Tests:

1. As previously stated, magnetite and pyrrhotite are attracted to a magnet. The latter more easily seen when powdered. Limonite-goethite, hematite, siderite, pyrite, and some other minerals containing small amounts of iron, when heated on charcoal with a blowpipe and alcohol lamp in the reducing flame, yield a magnetic

mass. If treated in this way pyrrhotite becomes more magnetic; whereas magnetite loses the ability to react to a magnet if heated, as above, but in the oxidizing flame. Equipment needed: a magnet, a rock crusher, a blowpipe and an alcohol lamp.

2. An iron mineral powdered, fused with soda on a charcoal block in the reducing flame and then boiled in a test tube with strong hydrochloric acid to which a few drops of nitric acid have been added will, upon the further addition of ample ammonia, yield a precipitate which is reddish brown in color. Equipment needed: a rock crusher, washing or baking soda, a charcoal block, a blowpipe, alcohol lamp, a test tube, hydrochloric acid (strong), nitric acid (strong) and ammonia.

Comments:

All the tests described are designed to show whether the element iron is part of the mineral specimen, thereby identifying it as an iron mineral (those that become magnetic when blowpiped on charcoal, due to the iron content). But iron minerals aren't a good prospect unless they are with copper (chalcopyrite) or nickel (pentlandite), or in large deposits.

In the county of Shropshire, England, my wife and I admired, photographed and walked across the first iron bridge ever constructed (more than 200 years ago) still proudly spanning the River Severn. It stands as a tribute to the durability of the metal when treated to withstand corrosion; it also serves as a reminder that the industrial revolution was born in the immediate area. Rust, the bane of most of us owning items made of iron exposed to moisture, is the good friend of a prospector. To discover an area of rocks and soil coated heavily with the corrosion, is like an answer to a prayer. Such a region is known as a gossan, or iron hat. It indicates a mineralized zone worth further investigation. Below could rest economically important minerals awaiting discovery.

See: how to make a small rock crusher, p.80; streak plates, p.79; how to make a charcoal block, p.60; how to make a blowpipe, p.63; how to make an alcohol lamp, p.73; diluting acids, p.81.

Zinc

Sphalerite is the principal ore of zinc. The name comes to us from *sphaleros*, the Greek word meaning treacherous. It is also called blende, from the German word *blenden*, meaning to deceive. From this one should gather that it's not the easiest mineral to identify. The most common zinc mineral is sphalerite which is often found with the lead mineral galena.

Zinc is used to plate objects that might rust, this is called galvanizing. When alloyed with copper the result is brass. Willemite, the zinc mineral, when part of a mixture of other minerals, can be easily overlooked; that is until subjected to short-wave ultraviolet light, when it will often fluoresce a brilliant green. This green is enhanced when accompanied by calcite fluorescing brilliant pinkish red. The willemite reaction is so distinctive, no further tests are required.

Visible properties: Sphalerite can range from colorless to white, yellow, green, red, brown and black; it is transparent to translucent. *Luster:* resinous to adamantine. *Hardness:* 3.5 to 4, brittle. *Streak:* variable, from white to yellow and pale brown.

Makeup: zinc (Zn) + sulfur (S); often including one or more of the following: iron (Fe), manganese (Mn), lead (Pb), cadmium (Cd), mercury (Hg), tin (Sn), silver (Ag), gold (Au), indium (In), gallium (Ga) and thallium (Tl).

Tests:

1. Since sphalerite is a sulfide, any specimen suspected of being the zinc mineral should be checked first to ensure it belongs to that group. A fragment is crushed to powder, put into a test tube with dilute hydrochloric acid, boiled and, if a sulfide, a smell of rotten eggs (hydrogen sulfide) is soon detected. This test quickly eliminates the look-alike mineral siderite, an iron carbonate, which would dissolve with effervescence and no odor. Equipment needed: a rock crusher, test tube, hydrochloric acid (dilute) and an alcohol lamp.

2. Once it has been established the mineral is a sulfide, crush another fragment to powder, combine it in equal parts with a 3 to 1 mixture of soda and powdered charcoal, add water to form a paste and with a blowpipe and alcohol lamp heat strongly in a reducing flame. If zinc is present a yellow coating will form on the charcoal, which upon cooling changes to white. As a double check: put a drop of cobalt nitrate onto the coating, heat it strongly in the reducing flame, and a green color should be seen. Just for fun I performed the above test, but added cobalt carbonate powder to the soda and charcoal powder. After I'd heated the assay and flux strongly, I put a drop of dilute nitric acid onto the mass, reheated and got the lovely green color. Equipment needed: a rock crusher, soda, powdered charcoal, a blowpipe, a charcoal block, an alcohol lamp and cobalt nitrate.

3. A few economically important zinc minerals, including sphalerite and especially willemite, fluoresce under short-wave ultraviolet light; but not all. Further tests should be performed on all fluorescing

minerals. Equipment needed: a short-wave UV lamp.

Comments:

A geology student to whom I confessed my difficulty in identifying this mineral by sight every time, said: "Me too! In the university whenever I'm given a tray of mineral specimens to name, those I don't recognize I put down as sphalerite—and I'm often right!"

As mentioned, an ultraviolet lamp is desirable for those searching for zinc minerals, because a uneconomic, nondescript, easily overlooked zinc carbonate, hydrozincite, is often found in the weathered zones of zinc deposits. This secondary, pathfinder mineral almost always fluoresces a brilliant blue.

See: how to use a streak plate, p.79; how to make a rock crusher, p.80; how to make an alcohol lamp, p.73; how to make a blowpipe, p.63; how to make a charcoal block, p.60; diluting acids, p.81.

Nickel

Pentlandite is the principal ore of nickel. It's commonly associated with pyrrhotite and nickeliferous-pyrrhotite. Canada is blessed with large deposits of nickel minerals, and leads the world in output. The mines of northern Ontario and the recent discovery of a huge deposit in Labrador should keep us ahead of the pack. Nickel is used as an ornamental and protective coating for other metals to prevent corrosion, it is also used in several alloys such as nickel steel (nichrome) and is used in coinage.

Visible properties: Pentlandite is a pale bronze-yellow. *Luster:* metallic. *Streak:* pale brownish bronze. *Hardness:* 3.5 to 4, brittle.

Makeup: Nickel (Ni) + iron (Fe) + sulfur (S).

Tests:

1. Pentlandite is nonmagnetic. It can be made magnetic by heating some of the powdered mineral with soda on a charcoal block in the reducing flame of a blowpipe and alcohol lamp. Equipment needed: magnet, rock crusher, baking or washing soda, charcoal block, alcohol lamp and blowpipe.
2. When a fragment is heated strongly on charcoal to eliminate the sulfur and powdered, and then a hot borax bead in the loop of a platinum wire touched to it will, upon reheating in the oxidizing

flame and if a nickel mineral, produce a violet-colored bead when hot; brownish—cold. Equipment needed: rock crusher, charcoal block, alcohol lamp, borax and blowpipe.

3. Powder another piece of the mineral (about the size of a pea), place into a test tube with a 1 to 1 mixture of nitric acid and water, and heat over an alcohol lamp until dissolved. Filter until the liquid is clear, then pour half into a second test tube. To the first test tube add a similar amount of ammonia and, if sufficient nickel is present, the liquid will turn a pale blue color. To the second test tube add a few drops of a dimethylglyoxime solution of the chemical mixed with alcohol (prepared several hours earlier) and, if nickel is there to react, a pale red precipitate is seen. Equipment needed: rock crusher, test tube, alcohol lamp, blowpipe, nitric acid (strong), water, ammonia and dimethylglyoxime solution.

Comments:

Along with the words Welsh and Prime Minister, the name nickel started out as a derogatory word. The reason: German miners of long-ago were very frustrated by the copper-colored mineral, niccolite, (calling it *kupfernickel*—copper nickel) which they believed was bewitched by a mischievous evil spirit, Nick, since it was difficult to smelt and gave no copper. It seems only fitting then, that an alloy containing copper and nickel is known as German silver. Nickel minerals exposed to weathering are sometimes found coated with light green annerbergite, a secondary nickel-arsenate mineral. This nickel bloom is of importance as a pathfinder mineral to what's further below the surface.

See: bead tests, p.74, how to make a rock crusher, p.80; how to make a charcoal block, p.60; how to make a blowpipe, p.63; how to make an alcohol lamp, p.73; diluting acids, p.81.

Cobalt

In Canada, several cobalt minerals are found, particularly in Ontario. In fact, there is a city in Ontario named for the area's surrounding deposits. The most important minerals are lumped together under the name tin-white cobalt, of which skutterudite is one. The other names given depend on the order of dominance of cobalt, iron and nickel in the arsenides. Cobaltite is another mineral not in the group, but it is difficult to distinguish from them. Cobalt is used in alloys to make tools to cut steel and is also alloyed with iron to produce permanent magnets.

Visible properties: Tin-white cobalt and cobaltite are both tin-white unless hidden by an iridescent tarnish. *Streak:* grayish black to black. *Luster:* metallic, opaque. *Hardness:* 5.5 to 6, brittle.

Makeup: Skutterudite (and others in the group)—cobalt (Co) + nickel (Ni) + iron (Fe) + arsenic (As).
Cobaltite—cobalt (Co) + arsenic (As) + sulfur (S).

Tests:

1. Possible cobalt minerals should first be powdered, heated strongly on charcoal with a blowpipe and alcohol lamp until all arsenic and sulfur has been driven off before a bead test with platinum wire is attempted. Then, form a borax bead in the loop of the wire, touch the powder with it until some adheres, and reheat in either the reducing flame or oxidizing flame. Hot or cold, in both flames, the identifying color is deep blue if cobalt is present. When making the bead test, try not to get too much powdered mineral onto the bead to prevent producing a blackish bead. Equipment needed: rock crusher, charcoal block, a blowpipe, alcohol lamp, borax and platinum wire.
2. Like nickel and iron minerals, cobalt minerals become magnetic if the first part of the above test is conducted; except soda is mixed with the powder before heating in the reducing flame. Equipment needed: as above but with soda.

Comments:

Erythrite, a secondary cobalt arsenate, is found in the weathered portions of cobalt ore deposits. This cobalt bloom, a pathfinder mineral and friend of a prospector, ranges from pinkish blue to deep reddish purple depending on whether nickel is present (former color) or cobalt dominates (latter color).

See: how to make a rock crusher, p.80; how to use a streak plate, p.79; how to make a charcoal block, p.60; how to make an alcohol lamp, p.73; bead tests, p.74.

Chromium

Chromite is the only economically important ore of chromium. Canada has some deposits of this mineral, mostly in the Canadian Shield country; yet they have only gained enough importance to mine during wartime. Chromium is used in chrome plating to prevent rusting, and also in alloys such as nichrome and chrome-vanadium for hand tools.

Visible properties: Brownish black to black. *Streak:* dark brown. *Luster:* submetallic. *Hardness:* 5.5, brittle.

Makeup: chromium (Cr) + iron (Fe) + oxygen (O).

Tests:

1. Chromite is sometimes slightly magnetic. If thus, it becomes more so after a fragment is heated in the reducing flame on charcoal. Equipment needed: magnet, charcoal block, alcohol lamp and blowpipe.
2. A borax bead in the loop of a piece of platinum wire when dipped into some of the finely powdered mineral and reheated again in the oxidizing flame shows a yellowish color hot and yellowish green when cold, for chromium. With further dippings into the powdered mineral and more heating, much finer greens are produced. If a change is then made to the reducing flame, the bead color is green either hot or cold. Equipment needed: borax, platinum wire, alcohol lamp, blowpipe and rock crusher.

Comments:

The colors imparted by chromium compounds are responsible for the greens of emeralds and the reds of rubies.

See: streak plates, p.79; bead tests, p.74; chemicals and how some are prepared, p.83; how to make a charcoal block, p.60; how to make a blowpipe, p.63; how to make a rock crusher, p.80; how to make an alcohol lamp, p.73.

Molybdenum

In some parts of the world and Canada molybdenite is an important ore of the element. Along with chromium, molybdenite is used to produce high-speed steel which is made into tools such as metal drill bits. It is also used in corrosion-resistant stainless steel.

Visible properties: Molybdenite is lead gray in color. *Streak:* blue-gray. *Luster:* metallic, opaque. *Hardness:* 1 to 1.5, sectile.

Makeup: molybdenum (Mo) + sulfur (S).

Tests:

1. Feels greasy to the touch.
2. Leaves a grayish green mark on paper (graphite, one of the only minerals with which it could be confused, also marks paper easily; but fails the following test). Equipment needed: a piece of white paper.
3. Molybdenum is decomposed by strong nitric acid, leaving a whitish to gray residue (graphite is unaffected by acids). Equipment needed: rock crusher, test tube, alcohol lamp and nitric acid (strong).
4. On charcoal with a blowpipe and alcohol lamp in the oxidizing flame, a red ring appears next to the assay with a yellow cooling to white coating nearby; plus sulfur fumes occur. Equipment needed: charcoal block, alcohol lamp and a blowpipe.
5. On a plaster of Paris block with potassium iodide flux, molybdenum gives a deep blue coating. Equipment needed: plaster of Paris block, blowpipe, alcohol lamp and potassium iodide flux.

See: streak plates, p.79; diluting acids, p.81; chemicals and how some are prepared, p.83; how to make a blowpipe, p.63; how to make a rock crusher, p.80; how to make an alcohol lamp, p.73.

Tungsten

Scheelite, wolframite and ferberite are tungsten minerals found in Canada; yet tungsten has only been processed here in a minor way. Tungsten-carbide is probably the most common steel-cutting alloy found in machine shops.

Visible properties: Scheelite is colored white, pale shades of green and brown, and reddish. *Streak:* white. *Luster:* vitreous to adamantine. *Hardness:* 4.5 to 5, brittle.
Wolframite and ferberite are blackish brown to black. *Streak:* close to black. *Luster:* submetallic. *Hardness:* 5 to 5.5, brittle.

Makeup: Scheelite—calcium (Ca) + tungsten in tungstate form (WO_4). Wolframite—iron (Fe) + manganese (Mn) + tungsten in tungstate form (WO_4).
Ferberite—iron (Fe) + tungsten in tungstate form (WO_4).

Tests:

1. Most possible tungsten minerals may be tested in the following way. Powder, fuse with soda on charcoal using the blowpipe and alcohol lamp (both wolframite and ferberite become magnetic), put the assay into a test tube with strong hydrochloric acid and boil. Upon the formation of a yellowish residue drop into the liquid either a snipping of tin or zinc and, if sufficient tungsten is present, the liquid will turn bluish with tin; bluish gray with zinc. Zinc is obtainable from the casings of defunct dry-cell batteries, galvanized iron scrapings. For tin, use a small snipping of tin solder. Equipment needed: rock crusher, sodium carbonate, charcoal block, blowpipe, alcohol lamp, test tube, hydrochloric acid (strong) and metallic tin or zinc.
2. Scheelite almost always fluoresces from yellow-cream to blue under short-wave ultraviolet light. An ultraviolet lamp is the recognized tool with which to prospect for the mineral. Equipment needed: short-wave UV lamp.

See: diluting acids, p.81; how to make an alcohol lamp, p.73; how to make a rock crusher, p.80; how to make a blowpipe, p.63; streak plates, p.79.

Manganese

Manganese is a common element found, in varying amounts, in a good number of minerals throughout North America. Pyrolusite and rhodonite are two good examples found in Canada. It is used chiefly in making steel.

Visible properties: Pyrolusite ranges from 1 to 6.5 in hardness; the latter figure only in crystals. *Luster:* metallic. *Streak:* black. *Color:* dark steel gray to black.
Rhodonite is usually some shade of pink. It rapidly weathers, however, to pencil-lead black. Pink material gives a white streak. Transparent to translucent and opaque. *Luster:* vitreous. *Hardness:* 5.5 to 6.5.

Makeup: Pyrolusite—manganese (Mn) + oxygen (O).
Rhodonite—manganese (Mn) + silicon in silicate form (SiO_3).

Tests:

1. Pyrolusite reacts in cold hydrogen peroxide with the evolution of oxygen. It dissolves in hydrochloric acid giving off chlorine: an

unpleasant smelling, rusty green, poisonous gas. With a platinum wire, blowpipe, alcohol lamp and soda, gives an attractive robin's egg blue bead when cold, after heating in the oxidizing flame. At the lower end of the hardness scale, it will soil fingers. Equipment needed: rock crusher, test tube, hydrogen peroxide, hydrochloric acid, platinum wire, blowpipe, alcohol lamp and soda.

Rhodonite is only easily identified by color, on fairly fresh surfaces, before weathering has taken place. It can be confused with another pretty pink manganese mineral, rhodocrosite, a carbonate, which is softer, at 4 on Mohs' scale of hardness.

Comments:

Pyrolusite is found as mosslike inclusions in chalcedony (moss agate). It also forms flattened, fernlike growths along cracks in rocks often, incorrectly, thought to be fossils. Rhodonite is a popular lapidary material. The second test for manganese was only included, in the event a piece of an unknown mineral, thought to be a carbonate, was dropped into a test tube with hydrochloric acid and, instead of fairly harmless carbon dioxide, chlorine gas was produced. If this ever happens, instantly terminate the test and dilute the test tube contents by immersing in a bucket of water.

See: streak plates, p.79; bead tests, p.74; diluting acids, p.81; how to make an alcohol lamp, p.73; how to make a blow pipe, p.; how to make a rock crusher, p.80.

Mercury

Mercury is the only liquid metal at ordinary temperatures and is the heaviest liquid known. Cinnabar is the principal ore of mercury. Canadian deposits of this mineral seem to have only gained importance during wartime, when other, cheaper sources, were unavailable. Mercury is used in thermometers, electric switches and dental fillings. It is also used by gold seekers to help gather together the gold in a gold pan.

Visible properties: Some shade of red from brick to bright, brownish red, and rarely lead gray. *Streak:* scarlet. *Luster:* adamantine to metallic, and dull in crumbly specimens. *Hardness:* 2 to 2.5, partially sectile.

Makeup: mercury (Hg) + sulfur (S).

Tests:

1. Cinnabar has a high specific gravity at 8.1; so, when a piece is held in one hand with a similar-sized piece of rock in the other, the added weight should assist identification.
2. Powder a small part of the suspected cinnabar, mix with 3–4 times the quantity of sodium carbonate, place into a pyrex test tube, cap and heat over an alcohol flame. If the element is present, a sublimate of metallic mercury will be seen. A fragment of possible cinnabar heated on a charcoal block with a blowpipe and alcohol lamp, will deposit onto a clean copper coin (held just over it with tweezers) a gray substance. To double check, squeeze a drop of dilute hydrochloric acid onto the gray mass, rub with a finger and, if it is in fact cinnabar, the copper will be coated silver-white. Equipment needed: rock crusher, washing soda, test tube, alcohol lamp, charcoal block, blowpipe, copper coin, tweezers, dilute hydrochloric acid.

Comments:

Mercury seems to have had bad press in the past few years, some of it deserved. Mercury vapor is a serious health hazard for workers breathing it. When working with it or an ore of the liquid metal, do so only in a well-ventilated area and for short periods.

About the only mineral reddish in color that cinnabar could be mistaken for is realgar, an arsenic sulfide. However realgar, like arsenopyrite, gives the characteristic garliclike odor—indicating arsenic, not mercury—when subjected to some tests.

See: how to make a rock crusher, p.80; how to make an alcohol lamp, p.73; how to make charcoal blocks, p.60; diluting acids, p.81; chemicals and how some are prepared, p.83.

Arsenic and Antimony

Both of these elements are found, in varying amounts, as part of the gangue in many minerals. Arsenopyrite is the arsenic mineral most often met with; stibnite is the most common antimony mineral. Since they're both sulfides, I've decided to lump them together.

Visible properties: The first mentioned is silver-white with a metallic luster, and a dark gray to black streak. *Hardness*: 5.5 to 6, brittle. The latter is steel gray also with a metallic luster, and leaves a lead gray to steel gray streak. *Hardness*: 2, sectile.

Makeup: Arsenopyrite—arsenic (As) + iron (Fe) + sulfur (S).
Stibnite—antimony (Sb) + sulfur (S).

Tests:

1. Either mineral, when powdered and fused with soda on a charcoal block by means of a blowpipe and alcohol lamp, will test positive for sulfur. If the fused mass is placed onto clean silver (I keep an old silver-plated spoon, with much of the plating worn off, for such tests), moistened and crushed, it will produce a tarnished spot. Arsenopyrite will give a good iron test (it becomes magnetic). See test one, p.22. Equipment needed: rock crusher, soda, alcohol lamp, charcoal block, blowpipe and a silver article.
2. A sliver of stibnite will melt in the flame of a candle. Equipment needed: charcoal block, blowpipe, candle or alcohol lamp.
3. When a piece of arsenopyrite is broken with a hammer, there is often a garliclike odor, as there is when heated on a charcoal block. Equipment needed: hammer.
4. If stibnite is suspected of being part of an ore sample, to make sure, put a large drop of liquid Drano (or a drop from a strong mixture of powdered Drano and water, i.e., water is added until powder won't absorb any more) onto the surface, leave for 2 to 3 minutes, then apply a drop of dilute hydrochloric acid. Antimony is present if an orange color is seen. Equipment needed: Drano, hydrochloric acid.

Comments:

Arsenopyrite isn't often mined in this country, except when it's found to contain gold. For this reason it's known as an important pathfinder mineral to those after the precious metal. Whereas antimony minerals are generally unpopular with prospectors. The reason—too much of the element downgrades the quality of the find, and leads to penalties being imposed on ores sent to smelters for processing.

Take care when using Drano, whether testing for antimony or unblocking a pipe. It is no respecter of one's hide, being caustic. Caustic comes from the Greek word *kaustos* meaning to burn.

See: streak plates, p.79; how to make an alcohol lamp, p.73; how to make a blowpipe, p.63; how to make a charcoal block, p.60; diluting acids, p.81; chemicals, p.83.

Bismuth

Although both bismuthinite and native bismuth are found in Canada, they're by no means common. I know of only one occurrence in a silver mine on the Camsell River, N.W.T. Elsewhere it is a minor economic mineral or native element in other mines. Bismuth is used in medicine and cosmetics. It is also employed in some alloys such as pewter, printer's type and Wood's alloy.

Visible properties: Bismuthinite is most often steel gray (closely resembling stibnite) with an iridescent tarnish. *Streak*: same as color. *Luster:* metallic. *Hardness:* 2, to some extent sectile.
Native bismuth is pale reddish silver in color and easily tarnishes. *Streak:* shining silver. *Luster:* metallic. *Hardness:* 2, sectile though brittle.

Makeup: Bismuthinite—bismuth (Bi) + sulfur (S); sometimes with copper (Cu) and iron (Fe).
Native bismuth—bismuth (Bi); with traces of arsenic (As) and sulfur (S).

Tests:

1. A fragment of either mineral fuses fairly easily with a blowpipe and alcohol lamp on charcoal, producing a yellow coating. As above with a mixture of potassium iodide and sulfur added to the fragment, gives a yellow coating with a brilliant red border. The same test substituting a plaster of Paris block for the charcoal, gives a chocolate brown coating with underlying red. This changes to orange-yellow and red on exposure to ammonia fumes. Equipment needed: blowpipe, alcohol lamp, plaster of Paris block, ammonia, potassium iodide flux and charcoal block.
2. Both minerals dissolve in hot nitric acid. Upon the addition of water, a white precipitate is thrown down. Equipment needed: nitric acid, test tube, water and alcohol lamp.

Comments:

Wood's alloy has a low melting point of 65°C (149°F). I have a small plug of a bismuth alloy in the safety valve of my hot-water tank. If, perchance, the water overheats and the valve fails to release the pressure, at a certain temperature below boiling point the plug melts and does the job instead.

See: streak plates, p.79; diluting acids, p.81; how to make a charcoal block, p.60; how to make an alcohol lamp, p.73; how to make a blowpipe, p.63.

Uranium

With the lessening of sabre-rattling among the so-called superpowers, the universal outrage generated from nuclear accidents and the problems involved in getting rid of nuclear waste, uranium doesn't garner attention the way it once did. Canada has one of the largest reserves of uranium ores, its main use is in atomic reactors. Uraninite, a mineral composed of uranium and oxygen, and pitchblende, a variety of uraninite, are found here.

Visible properties: Uraninite (pitchblende) is steel black to brownish black (pitch black). *Streak:* gray, brown and almost black. *Luster:* submetallic, pitch-like to dull, opaque. *Hardness:* 5 to 6, brittle.

Makeup: uranium (U) + oxygen (O).

Tests:

1. Very heavy in comparison to an ordinary rock of similar size (about 2.5 specific gravity), at a specific gravity of 9.4. It is about half of the specific gravity of gold at 19.3; and almost twice that of pyrite at 4.9 to 5.2.
2. With the borax bead in the loop of platinum wire, in the reducing flame, it is green hot or cold. In the oxidizing flame it is yellow to orange—hot; yellowish to brown—cold. The bead almost always fluoresces brilliant pale green in short-wave ultraviolet light. Equipment needed: borax, platinum wire, alcohol lamp, blowpipe and UV lamp.

Comments:

Uranophane, a soft, canary yellow-colored mineral associated with uraninite and pitchblende, and found at or near the surface of occurrences, is another pathfinder mineral. The crusty deposit, uranium stain, fluoresces faint greenish yellow.

See: bead tests, p.74; chemicals, p.83; how to make an alcohol lamp, p.73; how to make a blowpipe, p.63.

Tin

The principal ore of tin is cassiterite; the name coming from the Greek word for tin, *kassiteros*. Although found in Canada along with the rare tin-tantalum mineral, wodginite, this country isn't exactly overflowing with cassiterite deposits.

Visible properties: Cassiterite is found from pale yellow, gray, red, brown and black. *Streak:* off-white, grayish, brownish. *Luster:* greasy to adamantine, opaque to transparent. *Hardness:* 6 to 7, brittle.

Makeup: tin (Sn) + oxygen (O).

Tests:

1. Tin ore at 6.8 to 7.1 specific gravity is heavy in comparison to a common piece of rock of similar size (about 2.5 specific gravity); therefore, if one were to compare the two rocks the tin ore would be about three times as heavy.
2. On charcoal, powdered cassiterite mixed with soda and charcoal dust, dampened and heated in the reducing flame with a blowpipe and alcohol lamp, will reduce to metallic tin with a white coating nearby. Equipment needed: charcoal block, blowpipe, alcohol lamp, soda.
3. Pieces of the mineral placed into a test tube with fragments of metallic zinc (obtained from the outer casing of an expired flashlight battery) and some dilute hydrochloric acid, and boiled, become coated with a deposit of the zinc; which will brighten considerably after washing and rubbing briskly. Equipment needed: test tube, alcohol lamp, metallic tin and hydrochloric acid.

Comments:

Over 2,000 years ago, what is now known as the British Isles was then called the Cassiterides, because of the large tin deposits in the county of Cornwall. Tin oxide is used in lapidary for polishing purposes.

See: streak plates, p.79; diluting acids, p.81; chemicals, p.83; how to make a charcoal block, p.60; how to make a blowpipe, p.63; how to make an alcohol lamp, p.73.

Sodium, Potassium, Barium, Calcium and Strontium

These of elements have a common test, in that some minerals containing them give an alkaline reaction on treated turmeric paper, that is why they are lumped together. Halite and glauberite are well-known sodium minerals and are both used as forms of salt; carnallite and sylvite are known for potassium. Barite is the best-known source of barium (used as part of a substance that is ingested prior to intestinal x-rays). Calcite and gypsum are known for calcium (gypsum is what goes into wall board in houses); and celestite is known for strontium.

Visible properties: HALITE, or rock salt, has a vitreous luster, and is brittle. *Hardness:* 2.5. It ranges from colorless to white, and can have shades of yellow, red, blue and purple.
GLAUBERITE has a glassy luster. *Hardness:* 2.5 to 3, brittle. It is white to whitish yellow, and gray to reddish.
CARNALLITE is white, sometimes reddish white, and is brittle. *Hardness:* 2.5. *Luster:* shiny.
SYLVITE ranges from colorless to white, bluish and reddish yellow. *Luster:* vitreous. *Hardness:* 2, brittle.
BARITE has a glassy luster. *Hardness:* 2.5 to 3.5, brittle. *Color:* from white through yellowish, grayish, bluish, reddish, brownish to dark brown.
CALCITE ranges from colorless to white, and with shades of gray, yellow, green, blue, violet, brown to black. *Luster:* from vitreous to earthy. *Hardness:* 3, one of the minerals listed in Mohs' scale of hardness, brittle.
GYPSUM is found from colorless, white, pale tints and all the way to black when impure. *Luster:* earthy, glassy, pearly, silky and almost to vitreous. *Hardness:* 2. Another of the minerals mentioned in Mohs' scale.
CELESTITE comes colorless to white, light blue and reddish brown. *Luster:* glassy. *Hardness:* 3 to 3.5, brittle.
The common test is not the only feature the minerals of these five elements have in common, they also all give whitish streaks. All are comparatively soft, some will scratch with a thumb nail, all will scratch with a knife blade.

Makeup: Halite—sodium (Na) + chlorine (Cl).
Clauberite—sodium (Na) + calcium (Ca) + sulfur in sulfate form (SO_4).
Carnallite—potassium (K) + chlorine (Cl) + magnesium (Mg) + water (H_2O).
Sylvite—potassium (K) + chlorine (Cl); sometimes with sodium (Na).
Barite—barium (Ba) + sulfur in sulfate form (SO_4).

Calcite—calcium (Ca) + carbon dioxide (CO_2); sometimes with manganese (Mn), iron (Fe) and magnesium (Mg).
Gypsum—calcium (Ca) + sulfur in sulfate form (SO_4) + water (H_2O).
Celestite—strontium (Sr) + sulfur in sulfate form (SO_4).

Tests:

1. The common test mentioned previously is very easy to perform. Simply heat a fragment of the unknown mineral strongly on a charcoal block with a blowpipe and alcohol lamp, then place onto a piece of dampened turmeric paper. If one or more of the five elements are present in the specimen, a distinct reddish stain soon appears. Equipment needed: turmeric paper, water, blowpipe, alcohol lamp and charcoal block.

2. HALITE is readily identified by a salty taste; and confirmed by the intensely yellow flame, indicating sodium, produced when some of the powdered mineral is introduced into an alcohol flame. Equipment needed: rock crusher, iron wire, spectacle lens, alcohol lamp, water.
GLAUBERITE has a slightly bitter, salty taste and also gives a sodium yellow flame. On charcoal with a blowpipe and alcohol lamp, in the oxidizing flame, it fuses to a whitish bead. This bead will test positive for sulfur, by producing a tarnished spot on silver. Equipment needed: rock crusher, iron wire, spectacle lens, alcohol lamp, water and silver object.
CARNALLITE tastes bitter and salty and gives a beautiful violet flame, indicating potassium, unless obscured by the presence of sodium. To filter out the sodium flame it is necessary to look through a thick blue glass. Beads of water will form on the side of a test tube (held at an angle of about 45 degrees) when a fragment is heated in it over an alcohol flame. It is very thermoluminescent. More bitter than halite to taste; it doesn't give the sulfur test on silver like glauberite. Equipment needed: rock crusher, iron wire, spectacle lens, alcohol lamp, water, test tube, tweezers, and silver object.
SYLVITE provides the same violet flame of potassium, unless masked by sodium. Also more bitter than halite, it doesn't give the sulfur test on silver like glauberite; it is softer than carnallite and it doesn't release water when heated in a test tube. Equipment needed: rock crusher, iron wire, spectacle lens, alcohol lamp, water, test tube, hardness points and silver object.
BARITE provides the sulfur test on silver. A flame, yellowish green in color, occurs when fused on charcoal with a blowpipe and alcohol lamp. The fragment, so heated, often fluoresces orange under short-

wave ultraviolet light. It is insoluble in acids and sometimes emits an unpleasant odor when rubbed. Equipment needed: rock crusher, iron wire, alcohol lamp, water, UV lamp and silver object.

CALCITE dissolves in a test tube in dilute hydrochloric acid with effervescence. If a lighted match is held in the gas given off (CO_2), the flame will go out. If dilute sulfuric acid (from an old car battery) is then added, a precipitate of colorless white crystals, calcium sulfate (gypsum) appears. Calcite will often fluoresce; especially after intense heating on charcoal. It gives a reddish yellow flame with wire, alcohol lamp and hydrochloric acid. Equipment needed: rock crusher, hydrochloric acid, sulfuric acid, iron wire, spectacle lens, alcohol lamp, water, test tube and hardness points.

GYPSUM is scratchable with a fingernail. After powdering and boiling in dilute hydrochloric acid in a test tube (no effervescence), a few added drops of barium chloride solution will produce a white precipitate. A fragment heated strongly in the blowpipe flame will fluoresce under long-wave ultraviolet light. Gypsum reacts for calcium in a flame test; reacts for sulfur on silver. Equipment needed: rock crusher, hydrochloric acid, sulfuric acid, iron wire, spectacle lens, alcohol lamp, water, test tube, hardness points, UV lamp and silver object.

CELESTITE gives the sulfur test on silver. A crimson strontium flame is given off when tested with wire, in an alcohol flame. After intense heating, like carnallite, celestite shows thermoluminescence and also fluoresces. It is insoluble in acids. Equipment needed: rock crusher, hydrochloric acid, sulfuric acid, iron wire, spectacle lens, alcohol lamp, water, test tube, hardness points, UV lamp and silver object.

Comments:

Some of the minerals mentioned are only worth finding in large deposits. When one attempts to identify a mineral, it is often necessary to have the mind of a detective with a baffling case. The clues are there to find if one can uncover them. The minerals mentioned only reveal themselves after tasting, smelling, observing and scratching; and the need to subject them to tests with chemicals and equipment is usually necessary.

See: how to produce turmeric paper, p.83; taste tests, p.85; how to produce barium chloride, p.78; streak plates, p.79; how to make a rock crusher, p.80; diluting acids, p.81; flame tests, p.82; how to make a charcoal block, p.60; how to make an alcohol lamp, p.73.

Fluorine

The element fluorine is part of the composition of the mineral fluorite. From fluorite came the name fluorescence—that curious glowing capable of transforming certain nondescript rocks or minerals into objects of pure beauty. Fluorite is an attractive and fairly common mineral employed in industry; but, unfortunately, is usually too soft for jewelry.

Visible properties: Fluorite is found from colorless to white and through shades of yellow, green, blue, pinkish, crimson to brown. Some crystal specimens are composed of different colors. *Luster:* glassy. *Hardness:* 4, one of the minerals named in Mohs' scale of hardness, brittle. *Streak* is white.

Makeup: fluorine (F) + calcium (Ca).

Tests:

1. Fluorite often fluoresces when subjected to short-wave ultraviolet light, usually green or blue. Equipment needed: UV lamp.
2. In a darkened room when a small piece is held by tweezers into the flame of an alcohol lamp, briefly, then removed and held away from the flame, it commonly glows (thermoluminescence). Equipment needed: tweezers, alcohol lamp.
3. Reacts for calcium after a strongly heated fragment is placed onto damp turmeric paper. Equipment needed: charcoal block, water, blowpipe, turmeric paper and an alcohol lamp.
4. An interesting and very distinctive test is as follows. Drop some wax from a burning candle onto a clean sheet of glass, mark through it with a wooden skewer, toothpick or something that'll penetrate the wax without scratching the glass, drop into the depression some of the finely powdered possible fluorite and on top of that, a few drops of concentrated sulfuric acid, and leave overnight. In the morning, wash away the acid (without letting the hydrofluoric acid come in contact with clothing or flesh), remove the wax and, if the mineral contains fluorine, the mark made through the wax will be seen etched in the glass. Equipment needed: candle, small piece of window glass, wooden skewer, sulfuric acid and a rock crusher.

Comments:

Fluorite has excellent cleavage and the cleaved crystals, although soft, make interesting jewelry. Cleavage is an important identifying feature in some minerals, as is fracturing. With care, perfect octohedrons can be cleaved from it. A truly beautiful mineral, the colors often seem too good to be true. The test on turmeric paper, hardness and thermoluminescence should identify fluorite fairly easily. It's often better to be on the safe side when dealing with acids; safety glasses, plastic gloves and old clothes are advisable.

See: streak plates, p.79; how to make turmeric paper, p.84; how to make a rock crusher, p.80; how to make a blowpipe, p.63; how to make an alcohol lamp, p.73; how to make a charcoal block, p.60.

Phosphorus

The best-known mineral containing this element is apatite. Canada has apatite and phosphate deposits, mainly on the prairies, and also phosphate rocks, they are used mainly for fertilizer.

Visible properties: *Color:* ranges from colorless to white, several shades of green, brown, yellow, blue, violet and red. *Luster:* most often vitreous, from transparent to opaque. *Hardness:* 5, yet another mineral on Mohs' scale, is brittle. *Streak:* most often whitish.

Makeup: calcium (Ca) + phosphorus in phosphate form (PO_4); usually with either or both fluorine (F) and chlorine (Cl).

Tests:
1. A fragment held with tweezers before a blowpipe flame will color the flame orange. When moistened with dilute sulfuric acid (battery acid) the flame color is bluish green (indicating phosphorus). Equipment needed: tweezers, alcohol lamp, blowpipe and dilute sulfuric acid.
2. It dissolves, without effervescence, in hydrochloric acid, and yields a precipitate of calcium sulfate (gypsum) upon the addition of a few drops of dilute sulfuric acid (indicating calcium). If not already fluorescent reddish yellow in long-wave ultraviolet light, it will be after heating. Equipment needed: rock crusher, test tube, alcohol lamp, dilute hydrochloric and sulfuric acid, long-wave UV lamp.
3. When a chip is held in the side of an alcohol flame briefly, then away to view, it shows bluish white thermoluminescence. This is best seen in a darkened room. Equipment needed: tweezers and alcohol lamp.
4. If a portion of the powdered mineral is placed into a test tube with dilute nitric acid and heated until dissolved, upon the addition of an

ammonium molybdate solution and provided phosphorus is present, a yellow precipitate is thrown down. Equipment needed: rock crusher, test tube and nitric acid.

5. A simple field test involves placing a large drop of nitric acid onto the surface of a potential specimen, leaving it for awhile, then dropping some powdered ammonium molybdate onto the moistened spot. Phosphorus is indicated if the powder turns yellow. Equipment needed: nitric acid (dilute) and ammonium molybdate (powder).

Comments:

A beautiful mineral, although really too soft, it is sometimes used in lapidary.

See: streak plate, p.79; diluting acids, p.81; chemicals, p.83; how to make a blowpipe, p.63; how to make an alcohol lamp, p.73; how to make a rock crusher, p.80.

Lithium

Three rather complex lithium minerals, amblygonite, lepidolite and spodumene, are found in Canada. At various times they have been sources of lithium. It is used as a deoxidizer and for other uses not so benign such as nuclear weapons.

Visible properties: Amblygonite is colorless to white, brownish white, pale greenish white, lilac and blue-gray. *Streak:* white. *Luster*: greasy to glassy, transparent to translucent. *Hardness:* 5.5 to 6, brittle.
Lepidolite can be found white, light yellow, grayish, greenish gray, lilac and rose red. *Luster:* pearly to vitreous, transparent to translucent. *Hardness:* 2.5 to 4.
Spodumene is found transparent to translucent and opaque. *Luster:* pearly to glassy. *Streak:* white. It ranges from colorless to white, yellow, yellowish green, close to emerald green, buff and lavender. *Hardness:* 6.5 to 7.

Makeup: Amblygonite—lithium (Li) + aluminum (Al) + phosphorus in phosphate form (PO_4) + fluorine (F).
Lepidolite—lithium (Li) + potassium (K) + aluminum (Al) + silicon in silicate form (SiO_2) + fluorine (F) + water (H_2O).
Spodumene—lithium (Li) + aluminum (Al) + silicon in silicate form (SiO_2).

Tests:

1. On charcoal with a blowpipe and alcohol lamp, amblygonite fuses to a white sphere. This fluoresces white under short-wave ultraviolet light. Equipment needed: charcoal block, alcohol lamp, blowpipe, short-wave UV lamp.

   Lepidolite fuses glasslike on charcoal, with the flame a crimson color (lithium). The fused assay fluoresces pink or blue. It is a mica, so the cleaved plates are elastic. Equipment needed: charcoal block, alcohol lamp, blowpipe, short-wave UV lamp.

   Spodumene usually fluoresces orange under long-wave ultraviolet light. Reacts similarly to lepidolite on charcoal, with the fused mass fluorescing blue. Equipment needed: charcoal block, alcohol lamp, blowpipe, long-wave UV lamp.

2. All can be flame tested for lithium with an alcohol lamp, iron wire and dilute hydrochloric acid. However, the crimson flame of strontium is similar to that of lithium. To differentiate between them, strontium minerals most often react positive on damp turmeric paper. Equipment needed: charcoal block, alcohol lamp, blowpipe, iron wire, water, hydrochloric acid and turmeric paper.

Comments:

Spodumene (hiddenite and kunzite) and amblygonite provide materials for gem stones.

See: streak plates, p.79; flame tests, p.82; diluting acids, p.81; turmeric paper, p.84; how to make a charcoal block, p.60; how to make an alcohol lamp, p.73.

Rocks and Minerals Used in Lapidary

Like many serious collectors of rocks and minerals, my interest was peaked after finding agate, jasper and other types of chalcedony and chert on a beach. This curiosity has never waned, even on another beach, when it was snowing, with a cold wind blowing, and I was soaked up to my nethers by a sneaky, high wave with a sense of humor. I had my finds safely in a bag and that was all that concerned me. Yet, despite my interests widening somewhat, I still enjoy visiting beaches and sand bars though these days I usually return home with few treasures.

Chalcedony

Comes with a variety of names depending on color, inclusions and occasionally with local names ending in -ite to describe fairly common types found near rivers or communities. It is classed, rather pompously, as semiprecious; as if anything as naturally beautiful as some chalcedony should be downgraded to second class.

Visible properties: Mostly translucent; sometimes transparent. *Luster:* waxy. *Streak:* white. *Hardness:* 6.5 to 7. Its fracture is uneven, rough and sometimes conchoidal. Chalcedony comes in so many colors and shades it is impossible to name them all, however some of the more famous members of the family are listed below.
CARNELIAN: more of a cherry red color.
SARD: similar to carnelian but more reddish brown.
CHRYSOPRASE: from greenish yellow to apple green in color.
BLOODSTONE: also called heliotrope. Dark green with red spots.
AGATE: banded chalcedony. Agate is divided into two by the difference in colors: Onyx—black with white bands, Sardonyx—red with white bands.
MOSS AGATE: usually colorless, with inclusions like ferns, moss, trees.

Makeup: silicon dioxide (SiO_2).

Tests:

1. Some can be scratched with a quartz crystal. Equipment needed:

quartz crystal.

2. Some fluoresce under UV light (short-wave). But there are no really good tests to identify chalcedony, a person has to rely on their eyes. About the only other natural material that could fool a person is quartzite, a rock, when there are no impurities to color it. But a close inspection will reveal the many tiny fractures within, giving it a cloudy appearance. Equipment needed: short-wave UV lamp.

Comments:

To help show up chalcedony on a dry beach or river bar, carry a container of water equipped with a short hose and spraying mechanism and spray as you go. The desired specimens will show themselves if there are any to collect, unless covered with mud. On Moolack Beach, Oregon, my wife and I found some fossils (like snail shells) that over the course of time had filled with silicon dioxide, then the shells had mostly disintegrated. What we found were perfect casts of the insides of the shells, showing all the whorls, in chalcedony.

See: hardness points, p.59.

Chert

Chalcedony and chert are almost like two peas in a pod, in that there's very little difference between them. They are formed in the same way and they are both from the quartz family; that is why some experts think they should be grouped together. But there are some noticeable variations, mainly in color and in the fact that most chert is opaque and chalcedony is translucent or transparent. Color differences are brought about by impurities of up to 20 percent. Jasper and flint are well-known cherts. Basinite is a fine-grained, blackish jasper, used by goldsmiths as streak plates to test the purity of gold.

Visible properties: Mostly opaque, only translucent on the thinnest edges. *Luster:* often dull. S*treak:* white, yellow, red, brown. *Hardness:* 6.5 to 7. *Fracture:* jasper fractures splintery; flint fractures in a conchoidal fashion. Chert is found in many colors and shades, especially jasper. In fact jasper is rarely found as a single color; being spotted, striped and multicolored. It is often found on the same beaches and bars as chalcedony.

Makeup: silicon dioxide (SiO_2).

Tests:

1. There are no recognized tests that I know of. All a person can do is to go out and look, and learn to recognize it by color alone.

Comments:

Near Brandon, in the county of Norfolk, England, at a place called Grimes Graves, some flint mines have been excavated and are open to the public. It's like a trip back in time to about 4,000 years ago, when descending to where the stone age miners, using only antler picks, worked to get out the best quality flint for tools and weapons.

Opal

Opal is best described as chalcedony with water. Common opal, as its name implies, is the most often found. There's also fire opal and precious opal. It can have up to 20 percent water content. The water content can be lost over the years, and with it goes most of the opalescence.

Visible properties: Opal comes in a variety of colors. It is translucent to opaque mostly. *Luster:* glassy to resinous; streak is white. *Hardness:* 5.5 to 6.5 on Mohs' scale of hardness. Opal fractures in a mostly conchoidal fashion.

Makeup: hydrous silicon dioxide ($SiO_2 + H_2O$).

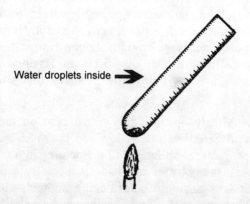

Water droplets inside ➡

Closed tube testing. So called, because added oxygen can't reach the fragment, as it would in open tube testing. The latter is a bent tube with both ends open, with oxygen flowing over the fragment held in the bend and heated from beneath.

Tests:

1. Will often fluoresce under UV light. All opal is easily identified by releasing water in a closed tube (chalcedony doesn't have any water to give up). Simply drop a fragment into a test tube held at 45 degrees over an alcohol lamp and heat strongly. If the specimen is opal, water droplets will collect on the upper, cooler side of the tube. Don't try this test with a specimen recently hauled from a river. Let it dry first. Equipment needed: test tube, alcohol lamp.
2. Opal can be scratched with a quartz crystal. Equipment needed: hardness points.

See: how to use a streak plate, p.79; hardness points, p.59; how to make an alcohol lamp, p.73.

Rhodonite

Rhodonite is a fairly popular lapidary material, usually carved or formed into cabochons (polished but uncut gems). As has been mentioned elsewhere, it has been mined for the manganese content. Sometimes found on the Fraser River bars.

Visible properties: For those wishing to find this mineral, think black not pink. Rhodonite rapidly weathers from a pink manganese silicate to a black manganese oxide. Where badly weathered, the black outer surface will soil fingers. *Streak:* white when a silicate. *Hardness:* 5.5 to 6.5. *Luster* is vitreous and it ranges from transparent to translucent.

Makeup: Pink rhodonite is very often found with black inclusions. Only the pink can be classed as manganese silicate ($MnSiO_3$), with minor amounts of iron (Fe) and magnesium (Mg).

Tests:

1. Again, think black; therefore the streak is not much help to a person looking for rhodonite. Any blackish (sometimes dark brown) rock thought to be hiding the pink stuff inside, can be easily identified as manganese oxide, by scraping off some of the exterior and conducting a bead test, with an alcohol lamp, blowpipe, platinum wire (or nichrome wire for manganese) and borax or washing soda flux. If there is a positive result, then sawing or splitting open will prove whether all the effort was worth it. Of course, one could be unlucky and find the rock had weathered to black all the way through.

Comments:

Pink feldspar is sometimes mistaken for paler pink rhodonite. Try breathing on the specimen, an earthy odor identifies it as a feldspar. See: bead tests, p.74; how to make an alcohol lamp, p.73; how to make a blowpipe, p.63.

Rhodocrosite

Another popular pink lapidary material, it can be confused with rhodonite. Found in Colorado, but the most important deposits are in Argentina. Rhodocrosite is a carbonate and another desired lapidary mineral.

Visible properties: *Hardness:* 4, almost too soft for jewelry. *Luster:* vitreous to pearly. *Streak:* white. It ranges from rose red to almost white in color and mostly striped, but quickly weathers to black with a streak of a similar color. Can be from translucent to transparent.

Makeup: manganese carbonate ($MnCO_3$).

Tests:

1. If the material in one's hand is striped in pretty shades of pink to almost white, and a fragment effervesces in a test tube with hydrochloric acid (dilute), held over an alcohol lamp at low heat, it's a good bet it's rhodocrosite. Acid has no effect on rhodonite.
2. To double check, try scratching with a knife blade. Rhodocrosite marks easily—rhodonite with difficulty or not at all. Can be bead tested for manganese. Equipment needed: hardness points.

See: acids and how to dilute, p.81; how to make an alcohol lamp, p.73; bead tests, p.74.

Rose Quartz

Not as popular as the preceding manganese minerals, but sometimes mistaken for them.

Visible properties: *Hardness:* 7. *Luster* is glassy, *streak* is white. *Color:* some shade of pink, due to impurities, and is transparent to translucent.

Makeup: silicon dioxide (SiO_2).

Tests:

    1. Won't test for manganese with a bead test and is only scratched by a quartz crystal with difficulty as it is at 7 on Mohs' scale.

    See: bead tests, p.74.

Orthoclase Feldspar

Another mineral, when pink, that is sometimes thought to be one of the manganese minerals. Very common.

Visible properties: *Hardness:* 6. *Luster* is glassy; *streak* is clear. *Color:* fleshlike when mistaken for the manganese minerals. Can be from transparent to translucent.

Left: Single orthoclase feldspar crystal.
Right: Carlsbad twin orthoclase feldspar crystal.

Makeup: Potassium aluminum silicate ($KAlSi_3O_8$).

Tests:

    1. Won't test for manganese with a bead test.
    2. When breathed on, releases an earthy odor.

Comments:

    Some feldspars are employed in lapidary.
    See: bead tests, p.74.

Thulite

Yet another mineral that has been mistaken for rhodonite, but is really a lapidary mineral in its own right. I have found it in Tunk Creek, near Riverside, Washington.

Visible properties: The pink variety of the mineral zoisite. *Hardness:* 6. *Luster* is glassy; *streak* is white; translucent. Can be found red, but is usually some shade of pink.

Makeup: hydrous calcium aluminum silicate (Ca_2Al_3 (Si_3O_{12}) (OH)).

Tests:

1. Sometimes fluoresces yellowish orange under UV light (long wave). Equipment needed: long-wave UV lamp.
2. Will test for aluminum, when heated on a charcoal block with a blowpipe and alcohol lamp. It fuses to a darkish mass the first blowpiping. Then a drop of cobalt nitrate is applied to the mass and reheated; a blue color indicates aluminum.

See: how to make charcoal blocks, p.60; how to make a blowpipe, p.63; how to make an alcohol lamp, p.73.

Turquoise

This is a beautiful mineral I have mixed feelings about. The reason—the first time I was called upon to identify a rough specimen as such at a rock and mineral show, I conducted a few tests and gave a positive reply. Several hours later I decided to check my procedure and results, and realized I had made a mistake and the specimen wasn't turquoise. I wasn't very happy about it. The problem is that many who want rocks and minerals identified, expect the results in a matter of minutes. That's not always possible if more than a guess is required. So to prevent feeling foolish in the future, I went to a shop selling rocks and minerals and bought several small, polished pieces for testing. Imagine my surprise when I found they were not turquoise either. I did further research on the subject and came up with the following: much turquoise sold is dyed; being porous, it is often treated with oil, wax or plastic to toughen it.

Visible properties: *Hardness:* 5 to 6. *Luster,* on a freshly broken surface, ranges from waxy to vitreous. *Streak* is whitish, often with darker spots in it. It ranges from apple green through blue-green to sky blue in color. Translucent only on thin edges.

Makeup: hydrous aluminum phosphate with copper
($CuAl_6 (PO_4)_4 (OH)_8 \cdot 5H_2O$).

Tests:

1. On a charcoal block with a blowpipe and alcohol lamp, a fragment, when heated, will attempt to commit suicide by jumping off the block.
2. In a test tube, heated over an alcohol lamp, the fragment almost explodes into pieces, turning brownish black. If the tube has been held at an angle of 45 degrees, water droplets will be seen on the upper, cooler side of the tube.
3. If a fragment, held in tweezers, is introduced into an alcohol lamp flame, it will color the flame green (copper).
4. If a drop of hydrochloric acid (dilute) is applied to the fragment, and the fragment reheated, the color changes to blue.
5. With chemicals, it will give a phosphorus test (see the test on p.42 using ammonium molybdate).

Comments:

Turquoise and the following mineral, chrysocolla, have both been copied by dying chalcedony blue. There are seven more minerals that resemble it to a greater or lesser degree.

See: how to make charcoal blocks, p.60; how to make a blowpipe, p.63; how to make an alcohol lamp, p.73; flame tests, p.82; diluting acids, p.81; chemicals and how some are prepared, p.83.

Chrysocolla

Chrysocolla is sometimes mistaken for and found intermixed with turquoise. A beautiful mineral not so often "tarted up" as is turquoise.

Visible properties: *Hardness:* 2 to 4. *Luster* ranges from dull, even earthy, to vitreous. *Streak:* very light green. *Color:* apple green to blue-green to sky blue and is opaque, though occasionally translucent. Some specimens are sectile.

Makeup: hydrous copper silicate (($Cu, Al)_2 H_2 Si_2O_5 (OH)_4 \cdot nH_2O$).

Tests:

1. Some specimens will stick to the tongue.
2. Won't give a positive test for phosphorus (helping to distinguish between it and turquoise).
3. Chrysocolla yields a copper globule if heated strongly on a charcoal block, using a blowpipe and alcohol lamp and washing soda flux, the flame is colored intense green—blue if a drop of hydrochloric acid is added. The fragment doesn't attempt to commit suicide (another difference between it and turquoise).
4. Chrysocolla quietly darkens and gives water in a closed tube, if the test tube is held at an angle of 45 degrees over the flame of an alcohol lamp (see p.46).

See: how to make charcoal blocks, p.60; how to make a blowpipe, p.63; how to make an alcohol lamp, p.73; chemicals and how some are prepared, p.83; diluting acids, p.81.

Howlite

This is a mineral I've had very little to do with. In fact I didn't know it existed until I did the research into turquoise and its imitations. Howlite is porous and dyes well to resemble turquoise. I'm sure there are people who have purchased dyed howlite in the belief they have turquoise.

Visible properties: *Hardness:* 3.5. *Luster:* ranges from very dull to a dull shine, so from opaque to almost translucent. *Streak*: white. *Color:* whitish, with darker veins (unless of course it has been dyed).

Makeup: silicoborate of calcium (Ca_2 B_5 SiO_9 $(OH)_5$).

Tests:

1. This borate fuses to a clear globule on a charcoal block with a blowpipe and alcohol lamp, coloring the flame boron green (not the emerald green of copper, as with chrysocolla).
2. A carpenter's nail will scratch howlite; but not turquoise.

Comments:

I can never look at a piece of turquoise today, without itching to test it with my hardness points, to check whether it is what it's supposed to be. But I must admit, dyed howlite makes very attractive jewelry.

See: hardness points, p.59; how to make charcoal blocks, p.60; how to make a blowpipe, p.63; flame tests, p.82.

Nephrite Jade

Nephrite jade is an amphibole mineral, the more sought after jadeite is a pyroxene (a group of silicate minerals). In British Columbia it's found on the Fraser River bars, when the river is low, in the depth of winter. When rockhounds, out on the bars after the green stuff, speak of their plumbing getting frozen, they're not talking about the water pipes in their homes.

Visible properties: It belongs near the darker end of a series of related members, commencing with tremolite which is white, to actinolite, a dark green. As well as the desired nephrite, between it and tremolite is another family member, the violet-colored hexagonite. Nephrite is compact and tough, more so than jadeite, and is used to make jewelry and for carving. Not being an expert, I'm not sure where nephrite begins and ends between the two end members. It seems to me that it should always be some shade of green, but is listed as also white, grayish, yellowish, reddish and brownish. Is white nephrite actually tremolite? And hexagonite thought of as violet nephrite? I don't suppose it really matters, so long as the finder is happy with the find. However, all family members have a *hardness* of 5 to 6 on Mohs' scale, so they can be marked with a quartz crystal.

Makeup: calcium magnesium (iron) silicate $(Ca_2(Mg, Fe)_5(Si_4O_{11})_2(OH)_2)$. The iron is absent in tremolite, but becomes very much a factor the nearer it gets to actinolite.

Tests:

1. Thin tremolite slivers will fuse to white glass; actinolite slivers fuse to black glass on charcoal with a blowpipe and alcohol lamp; darker specimens, with more iron, are easier to fuse.
2. The only identifying feature I know of, other than hardness, color and fusibility, is that nephrite has a hackly fracture. If you think of the way metal tears, leaving fine, short, sharp points on the broken surface, that's like a hackly fracture on rough rock. On river-tumbled specimens it's more difficult to notice, since you can't run your hand over the surfaces and feel the sharp points dig into the flesh. With those specimens visual identification is the key. On the smooth surfaces the fractures appear as lighter, wavy lines, at times not unlike the side views of saw blades, this is best seen under

magnification. This is one fracture of prime importance to learn where nephrite jade is found. Ask an experienced rockhound to show you a specimen with a hackly fracture. Equipment needed: magnifying glass.

See: how to make charcoal blocks, p.60; how to make a blowpipe, p.63; how to make an alcohol lamp, p.73.

Vesuvianite

In the book *Guide to Rocks and Minerals of the Northwest*, by Stan and Chris Leaming, published by Hancock House, it states that vesuvianite, also known as idocrase, can be found on the Fraser River bars. I have only seen a couple of pieces, but have never had the pleasure of testing some fragments. Yet I've read up on the silicate and this may help anyone trying to identify it.

Visible properties: *Hardness:* 6.5. *Luster* is glassy. *Streak* is white, transparent to translucent. *Color:* greenish, yellowish, yellow-brown.

Makeup: a complicated calcium aluminum silicate
$(Ca_{10}\ Mg_2\ Al_4\ (SiO_4)_5\ (Si_2O_7)_2\ (OH)_4)$.

Tests:

1. A fragment fuses easily, bubbling, to a darkish green or brown glass, before the blowpipe on a charcoal block with an alcohol lamp.

See: how to make a blowpipe, p.63; how to make charcoal blocks, p.60; how to make an alcohol lamp, p.73.

Porphory

Porphory is commonly found naturally tumbled smooth on some river bars and ocean beaches. In the dictionary it is described as rock consisting of a compact felspathic base, through which crystals of a different color are disseminated. I couldn't have put that better. Those rocks with smaller crystals (known as phenocryst—minerals of large dimensions compared to the size of rock particles they are in) are much more desirable than rocks with larger crystals.

Visible properties: The crystals are often softer than the rock they're in, so the rock is probably from 6.5 to 7 in hardness. *Luster:* I've found them generally dull. The smaller and fewer crystals there are, seems to indicate a better rock for polishing. *Color:* ranges from grayish white, brown, green and dark green to blackish, with the crystals usually of a lighter color. *Streak:* probably whitish, the streak isn't necessary to identify porphory. It is opaque.

Tests:

There aren't any tests of which I am aware. But once seen, porphory can always be recognized afterward.

Comments:

One has only to find a piece of porphory on a bar, with squarish feldspar crystals embedded, to wonder what they look like when free of rock. This is easily answered by leaving the Fraser River bar, and traveling east to Penticton. Once in Penticton head west along the Green Mountain Road. Not far past the Indian reserve, on the south side of the road, orthoclase feldspar crystals can be coaxed from the rock, including twinned orthoclase crystals known as Carlsbad twins. Because the igneous rock cooled slowly in that region there are large crystals throughout the area and therefore the feldspar crystals are easier to get out of the rock.

Obsidian

Also known as volcanic glass, obsidian looks the way it does because it cooled so rapidly crystals weren't able to form (unlike porphory, that cooled much slower, hence the crystals). Found in a number of places in the Pacific Northwest, probably the most famous occurrence is Obsidian Cliff in Yellowstone National Park, Wyoming.

Visible properties: *Hardness:* 5 to 5.5. *Luster:* vitreous. Inclusions can cause it to have a silver or golden sheen. *Color:* grayish, greenish, brownish and blackish. *Streak:* white, transparent mostly with conchoidal fracture.

Makeup: variable, a siliceous rock (Si).

Tests:

There are really no tests for this rock. The glassy look and the conchoidal fracture that produces razor sharp edges instantly identifies obsidian.

Comments:

Treat this rock the way you would broken glass.

Petrified Wood

Also known as fossilized wood, agatized wood, jasperized wood and opalized wood, this wood has the mineral composition of chalcedony, chert or opal. Wood becomes petrified over thousands and thousands of years. The petrification process occurs when organic matter, in particular cellulose, is converted into stone through the infiltration of water containing dissolved mineral matter (i.e., silica, calcium, carbonate). Petrified wood is fairly common, though not all specimens are suitable for grinding and polishing. Those found naturally tumbled on river bars and ocean beaches often provide the best specimens, as they have proven they are tough and hard by not disintegrating. My wife and I have always enjoyed finding and examining the petrified myrtle wood on Bullard's Beach, Oregon. There always seems to be a fresh supply cast up every day. Also, there's some interesting petrified wood on a dump at Coalmont, B.C.

The cell-like structure of bone, much enlarged

Visible properties: Petrified wood comes in a wide range of beautiful colors, with the patterns of the original wood often well preserved. Don't be fooled by hard, river- or ocean-tumbled sedimentary rock with well-defined bands. They were put there for you to find, just to make life difficult. *Hardness:* 6.5 to 7. (The 6.5 to 7 is for those specimens tumbled by rivers or the sea. Others I've checked are softer and not suitable for lapidary use.) *Luster:* dull to shiny. *Streak:* mostly white, but could be slightly colored; opaque.

Makeup: silicon dioxide (SiO_2).

Tests:

There are no real tests. It's simply a matter of learning to identify it with the eyes.

Comments:

Petrified bone is sometimes found where petrified wood occurs, especially on the Oregon coast, and could be mistaken for it until a closer look is taken. Most petrified bone that my wife and I have found came with much of the rock in which it was petrified adhering to it. This is not usual with sea-tumbled petrified wood. Also the cell-like structure of the bone is vastly different, as shown, to that of the wood, when viewed under low magnification.

Amber

About 50 million years ago the resin in pine trees started a process that has resulted in what is today called amber. Though not a mineral, the translucent fossilized resin offers persons interested in lapidary another material to work with. My wife, children and I collected some years ago, from a dump near Coalmont, B.C.

Visible properties: *Hardness*: 2 to 2.5. *Luster:* resinous, but polishes well. *Color:* it comes in a wide range of colors; but I've only found it in an orange yellow.

Makeup: $C_{10}H_{16}O$. Put another way, it is a mixture of resins.

Tests:

No tests are really necessary; but will burn. When rubbed with a cloth amber becomes electrically charged and will attract tiny particles to it. Kids enjoy playing with it.

Comments:

The earliest gem material used by man.

Pearl

Pearls are another natural creation that some might think unsuitable for this book. However, one of the largest pearls in the world, weighing in at 450 carats (about 2 pounds), is displayed in the South Kensington Geological Museum, in England; so, someone must have thought it belonged with rocks and minerals. In the U.S., the reputed largest pearl in the world is a hefty 14 pounds (6.37 kg). There are a variety of mollusks that produce pearls. I once met a man who'd found them in mussels, in Scotland. I found a pearl the way many have found them—by almost breaking a tooth on one.

Visible properties: *Hardness:* 3 to 4. *Luster:* dull to pearly. *Color:* ranges from white, silver, through cream to green, blue and black; is translucent to opaque.

Makeup: calcium carbonate ($CaCO_3$ and up to 12 percent organic matter and up to 4 percent water), similar to the mineral aragonite; and similar to the crust found inside kettles, in hard water regions, from the calcium.

Tests:

1. They will effervesce in most acids. Equipment needed: test tube, acid.
2. A natural or cultured pearl can be identified from a man-made imitation, by gently rolling it against the cutting edge of a front tooth. The artificial pearl will feel smooth; the natural or cultured variety have tiny ridges that can be detected.

Comments:

Fossil pearls have been found in fossilized mollusks. I know of at least one found in B.C. by Peter Thorne, a fellow contributor to the old *Canadian Rockhound Magazine.*

There are other rocks and minerals used in lapidary, but too many to include here. When purchasing lapidary rocks and minerals, especially those polished and part of jewelry, remember the short-sighted Roman gentleman who purchased a mule on a very dark night. Then, in the morning discovered the animal only had three legs. "I should have recalled the Latin phrase, *caveat emptor,*" he said to himself...let the buyer beware!

Identifying Equipment and Tests

Hardness Points

Hardness points are a collection of materials used to gauge the hardness of minerals by using Mohs' scale of hardness. Based on the fact that different minerals have differing hardness and that a mineral of a higher number on the scale will mark all those listed below it, the points can be used as effective tools for determining what a mineral's relative hardness is. Mohs' scale uses ten specific minerals and goes from softest to hardest with talc at number 1 and diamond at number 10.

A set of hardness points is fairly easy to make and is ideal for use in the field. Unfortunately, some of the minerals on the scale easily cleave, are very brittle or are expensive. To overcome these problems, I have used less fragile and very common materials as substitutes for the correct minerals. They are as follows:

Mohs' minerals	Substitute materials
1–talc and 2–gypsum	your fingernail, measuring just over 2
3–calcite	copper nail
4–fluorite	ordinary building nail
5–apatite	nail file
6–orthoclase	knife blade at 5.5 and a steel file at 6.5
7–quartz	small crystal
8–topaz	a piece of larger crystal
9–corundum	tungsten carbide at 9.125
10–diamond	nothing, if the mineral scratches 9 then it probably is diamond.

To hold my points I use a number of 2-inch lengths of 1/4-inch (6 mm) copper tubing. I flatten one end of each tube, about 1/4 inch and drill a hole through the flattened end. The various point materials are inserted into the other end of the tubing (slotting and opening up the tubing to suit); the points are then glued or lead soldered firmly in place. To complete the job I threaded the holes in the flattened ends onto a key ring. Finally, I magnetize the tip of the knife blade for testing the few magnetic minerals.

Hardness Test

Mohs' scale of hardness, although not precise enough for laboratory use, is ideal for testing in the field. It is based on the fact that a mineral of a higher number on the scale, will mark (scratch) all minerals that fall below it on the scale, so its relative hardness can be determined. For example, if a mineral will easily scratch calcite, but is itself readily scratched by apatite, then it must have a hardness between 3 and 5. It could be fluorite at 4. However, if the mineral marks calcite easily, but apatite with difficulty, it probably has a hardness of 4.5 to 5. The reason that it could possibly be a 5 is that minerals of the same hardness can mark each other. If this were not so, diamond dust could not be employed to grind diamonds. Like all testing methods, practice is required to become proficient.

Charcoal Blocks

A charcoal block is required during many identifying tests, along with an alcohol lamp and a blowpipe. A mineral specimen held in the depression of a block can be subjected to high heat. The heat comes from the flame of an alcohol lamp which is subjected to air being blown from a blowpipe. Charcoal blocks aren't too difficult to make if the following directions are closely heeded.

In *A Textbook of Mineralogy* by Edward Dana and William Ford, it states that charcoal blocks are best made from willow, pine or basswood. That's good to know—if one can recognize these trees. So, before launching into an explanation of how to produce charcoal, here are descriptions of the trees. Willows are common trees over much of North America. The lance-shaped leaves, 3 inches to 6 inches long (76 mm to 152 mm), easily identify most of them. If a person examines a weeping willow (the willow of the Bible and a common ornamental tree found throughout the world), they should recognize many willows that do not weep, but whose branches stick up and out. There are about 75 species on this continent, many of which are native to Canada. They are found around creeks, rivers and other wet locations.

Pines are easy to distinguish from other conifers. The long, thin needles and well-formed cones are the features to look for. Of the 35 species found in North America, 10 are native to Canada. They can be divided into soft (white) and hard (yellow); the former having 5 needles to a cluster; the latter having 2–3. One or more of Canada's 10 native pines are found in every province.

The basswood of North America is related to the lime of England and the linden of Germany. Here, in Canada, we have one native species of basswood. It is found from southern Manitoba eastward to New Brunswick. One of the European lindens is often planted along streets and can be looked for throughout the country. It has a heart-shaped leaf with one lobe larger than the other. These leaves and the flowers (and later the fruit), a cluster of which are attached to a single stalk which is also attached to a leaflike bract, make lindens and basswoods easy to identify.

Basswood leaf and fruit.

Hard and soft pine needles.   Open pine cone.

Charcoal is produced from wood in a retort (a sort of pressure cooker) by a process called destructive distillation; so, the next necessity is a retort. My first retort was made from a tobacco can and it served reasonably well, but required replacing regularly. I decided to make one that would last indefinitely using steel pipe fittings. I found an old, 3-inch (76 mm) pipe coupling (so-named because it joins 2 pieces of 3-inch diameter pipe, it is about 4 inches in length) and pipe plugs to screw into the coupling's ends. I welded a bar across the square head of one plug, to make it simpler to put together and take apart; on the square head of the other plug I welded a ring, to make it easier to put in and hook out of the fire. The concave ends of the pipe plugs made it possible to fit the 4-inch-long (10 cm) wood blocks snugly into this retort. Now, with the charcoal maker ready, the wood cut to size (4 inch x 1 inch x 1 inch), and the fire burning well, here is the final step. Wait until the fire is a mass of glowing coals. Put the wood into the retort and tighten the plugs just enough so they are easy to undo without having to use a wrench. Place the contraption into the fire and heap the coals about it, leaving a small section of the cap in view. The reason: as the gas is driven from the wood, it will be seen being forced from between the screw threads of the retort, the amount of gas and the speed with which it is evacuated depends on the heat of the fire.

A retort.

Once all the gas has been expelled, the charcoal is ready (unfortunately, there is no set time limit). Then hook the retort out of the fire, cool rapidly and it's ready for the next batch. If by chance the retort is left in the fire much after the gas has ceased emerging, the charcoal becomes brittle and breaks into small, useless pieces. If the fire is used before it is ready (before it is a mass of glowing coals), the smoke will mask the gas as it is expelled from the retort, and there will be no way of knowing when it ceases. In the event a charcoal block is required and a person hasn't time to indulge in the above exercise to obtain one, as a stopgap, simply take a piece of hand-sized wood, make a small depression in the end where the assay is to be blowpiped, and char most of that end well with a propane torch or other source of hot flame.

At one time I used to make my charcoal once a year, during the fall, on an open fire in the garden, when burning the prunings from my trees and other combustible items. If the day was fine, it was possible to get a very hot fire. Now, alas, since there is an outside burning ban in my home city, I can no longer produce charcoal this way. When my dwindling supply is finally used up, I shall be reduced to buying my charcoal blocks from a hobby store, although I have never seen them there. Some gem and mineral stores do however carry them.

Plaster of Paris Blocks

These pieces of testing equipment are easy to produce and are used in the same fashion as charcoal, but they are not a substitute for charcoal blocks. The charcoal is used for the majority of tests because many of the resulting coatings are white or pale yellow which do not show up well on the plaster; and because the charcoal blocks produce more heat, the reactions are stronger. However, some mineral elements such as selenium, cadmium and tellurium, show their identifying colors much clearer on these blocks.

The blocks should be approximately 1 1/2 inch x 1 1/2 inch x 4 inch (38 mm x 38 mm x 100 mm) long. Buy a package of plaster of Paris from a hobby store or wherever else it is available, dump into a container and make a fairly stiff mixture with water. Spoon into an oiled baking pan, then, before it dries, cut to shape with a knife. Another alternative is to locate an ice-cube tray with removable, soft plastic inserts making double ice cubes, and spoon the mixture into them. I can make 5 blocks at a time in this way and, since the blocks are easy to remove, there is no need for oil.

Some elements should be mentioned here, in the event they're encountered during testing, without flux, on a plaster of Paris block. When heated in the reducing flame of a blowpipe and alcohol lamp on the plaster cadmium (Cd) yields a greenish yellow with a hint of brown coating. Selenium (Se) produces a red coating, and usually a disagreeable odor described as similar to decaying horseradish. Tellurium (Te) provides a dark brown coating. These elements obviously show up better on the white background rather than the charcoal background.

Blowpipe

A blowpipe is a most necessary tool when bead testing with a platinum wire and a flux, or when heating a mineral fragment on a charcoal block or plaster of Paris block. It is used to test minerals for their elements by increasing the heat of the alcohol lamp flame and directing it onto the specimen being tested, this is done by blowing air through the pipe. But it takes a little practice to learn how to keep up a steady flow of air through the pipe while breathing through the nose. If one can't be bought, a blowpipe is fairly easy to fabricate.

Prior to the BIC pen company changing the tips of their ballpoint pens to predominantly plastic, very good blowpipes could be fabricated from them. I made one (and still have it) when I misplaced my regular blowpipe. Now, on the off chance someone has an old BIC pen they wish to convert, or another make with an all-metal end, here's how. Remove the metal end from the inner and outer plastic tubes, file the tip of the pen to extract the little ball, drill a hole in the side of the outer plastic tube, three-quarters of an inch from one end. This hole should be of a size so that the rear of the metal end fits in it snugly, and plug the end just below the hole with paper, chewing gum, etc. See drawing.

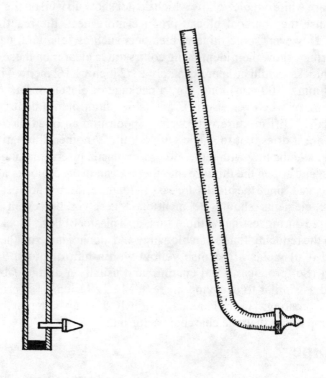

Left: BIC pen blowpipe; Right: Copper tubing and grease fitting blowpipe.

A blowpipe can also be produced from an 8-inch length (204 mm) of 1/4 inch (6 mm) copper tubing, a 1/16 inch (2 mm) grease fitting and some lead solder. Slot one end of the tubing and pry far enough apart so that the fitting can be screwed into it. Grind the back of the fitting until the little ball and spring inside pop out. Screw the fitting into the tubing and seal all around, also along the slots, with solder. It will then be found that the hole in the grease fitting is too large. To reduce the size, solder over the hole and force a tiny needle, no larger than 1/32 inch (less than 1 mm), through the solder. Finally bend at almost a right angle the end of the tubing with the fitting, approximately 1 1/2 inch (38 mm) from the end. Test for leaks by placing a finger over the tiny hole and blowing through the other end.

Turquoise
Turquoise from the southern U.S.

Rhodonite
Rhodonite from Salt Spring Island, B.C.

Copper Mineral
A specimen showing copper minerals. King Solomon Mine, Greenwood, B.C.

Copper Minerals
Left: A weathered specimen, that likely used to be chalcopyrite, showing where the iron in it has corroded and released the copper to form the secondary mineral (possibly malachite) underneath.
Right: Malachite specimen, a secondary copper mineral.

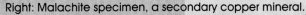

A chalcedony nodule.
Neptune Beach, Oregon.

Chalcedony
Half a chalcedony nodule, with
quartz crystals lining one of the
cavities. From a river bar in
Oregon.

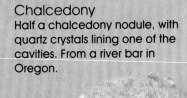

'Snake-skin' agate
(chalcedony). Oregon.

Flint Nodule
Flint, a variety of chert, is noted for
losing water from the surface,
leaving a porous coating of white
silica. This specimen is from Kent,
England.

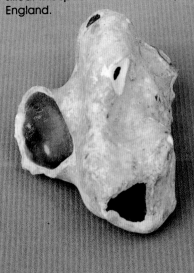

Porphory
Notice the squarish feldspar
crystals known as phenocrysts.
From a Fraser River bar.

Petrified wood specimens.
Coalmont & Oregon, B.C.

Petrified Wood
Rear specimen from Coalmont, B.C. The other three, sea tumbled, from Oregon. The front specimen given further tumbling by a tumbler to give it a polish.

Petrified bone. Oregon.

Cinnabar
Source unknown. Used purely to demonstrate mercury tests.

Bornite
A copper mineral showing the tarnished surface color. Specimen from Camsell River region of the N.W.T. Found with silver and bismuth.

Fluorite
Fluorite cleavage crystals.

Magnetite
An iron mineral shown here with the attraction to a magnet.

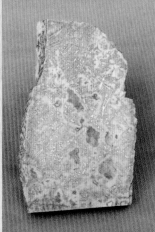

Native Silver
A slab of native silver ore from Camsell River. The silver is in calcite. Specimen from Northwest Territories, Canada. Back side of specimen shown at right, polished with emery cloth to remove the tarnish from the silver.

Chalcopyrite
This specimen is from the old Britannia Beach copper mine, where the author once worked.

Hematite
As shown below, hematite comes in many colors but always produces a red streak on a streak plate.

Galena Minerals
Galena is a lead mineral from the Kootenays, B.C.

Hardness Points
A set of hardness points. The magnet is housed in the aluminum cylinder.

Scratch Test
The author shown using the hardness points described above.

Acid Test
To determine if an article is solid silver or silver plated, a drop of dilute nitric acid is placed on a scratch. It won't attack silver but will attack the copper alloy beneath, if plated. The green color, indicating copper, will change to blue with the addition of a drop of ammonia.

Flame Test
Flame test for copper. The blue coloring is obtained if hydrochloric acid is employed as the moistening agent.

Streak Tests
Three different varieties of hematite, an iron mineral, three different hardnesses. But all give a reddish streak when drawn across a streak plate.

Basic Test Kit
Small enough to fit in one's pocket, this kit contains a set of hardness points, a streak plate and eraser, a magnet, and a 10x magnifier with a shoelace to hang around your neck.

Average Test Kit
The same set as described above may include a dropper bottle of hydrochloric acid for those responsible (or brave) enough to carry acid.

Professional Test Kit
Here is a light, compact set for field trips. Contents include: a bent wire used as a test tube holder, home made tweezers, a candle in a small can, a simple rock crusher, a spectacle lens, platinum wire, twist ties, a charcoal block, hydrochloric acid, washing soda, borax, cobalt nitrate, treated turmeric paper, fragments of tin and zinc, and a mixture of sulfur and potassium iodide.

Rock Crushers
Three types of rock crushers. My favorite is on the left, which I made out of steel, a pestle and mortar. Although too heavy to carry around with me, I use it in preference to the others at home.

Splitting Tools
A heavy hammer, two sharp chisels and a gad (pointed chisel on the right) are available at most hardware stores. A strong backpack is also required, available at most army surplus stores.

Chiseling a chip from a larger specimen will reveal an unweathered surface which is usually easier to identify.

Here the author is seen using a 10x magnifier to closely examine a rock's crystal structure.

Stream beds are an excellent source for mineral collecting as rock from miles around is washed down to river bars, creating a great variety of specimens.

I once had the pleasure of watching a goldsmith from Idar-Oberstein, West Germany, producing jewelry, and was somewhat surprised to see him use a blowpipe to solder the pieces together.

Alcohol Lamp

Without an alcohol lamp or candle, the charcoal blocks, wires and test tubes would be useless because much of mineral testing requires a source of heat. If you aren't able to buy one, read on.

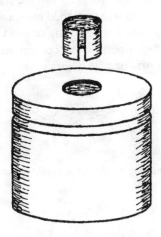

Alcohol lamp (not to scale).

Much more efficient than an ordinary candle, an alcohol lamp is both cheap and easy to make. Procure a small glass jar with a metal lid (steel— not aluminum; test with a magnet) such as one that has held green olives; or any small jar with a wide bottom that is not readily knocked over. Punch or drill a 1/4 inch (6 mm) hole through the center of the lid. Cut a piece of sheet metal 3/4 inch x 3/4 inch (19 mm x 19 mm) square from a bean or soup can (also not aluminum), bend around a 7/32-inch (5 mm) drill bit to form a tube, and solder the seam. Push the tube just through the hole in the lid, and solder into place. Purchase a lamp wick (or locate some thick felt and cut a strip to suit) and, with a piece of fine wire wrapped around one end, pull the wick through the tube until about 3/16 inch (5 mm) is left showing. Then buy a can of methyl hydrate from a hardware store, half fill the jar, and the lamp is ready to go. The only thing required to fully complete the lamp is a little cap to fit over the wick, to prevent the alcohol from evaporating when not in use. Failing that, always empty the alcohol out of the lamp.

Bead Tests and Reducing and Oxidizing Flames

Bead tests occur when a mineral and a flux are heated over an alcohol lamp in the loop at the end of a piece of platinum wire. The tests are so named because the melted flux (a mixture that is used in combination with powdered minerals and heat to fuse with and identify minerals) resembles a bead. During a bead test the wire is heated and dipped into a flux (i.e., baking soda, borax, salt of phosphorus). Then the flux on the wire is heated and turns into a bead, the bead is then dipped into the powdered mineral and everything gets heated again. The resulting colors that appear should then give a clue as to what the mineral is, as certain minerals in combination with certain fluxes give off specific colors.

Blowpiping a bead in the oxydizing flame.

Blowpiping with a charcoal or plaster of Paris block in the reducing flame, and the positions of the coatings.

Oxydizing flame and reducing flame.
The arrows point to where the bead or mineral fragment should be heated.

Bead tests and those tests conducted on a charcoal block are the backbone of mineral testing. But don't attempt any tests requiring a blowpipe and alcohol lamp until proficiency has been reached at producing reducing and oxidizing flames. The secret of making successful bead tests and other tests involving charcoal and plaster of Paris blocks, rests solely on the tester being able to produce these flames with a blowpipe and alcohol lamp (or a candle).

For the reducing flame the tip of the blowpipe is held just outside of the flame (as shown), and the flame is redirected to the side, onto the specimen under test, by blowing steadily through the pipe. The gases of the hot flame take oxygen from the test object, resulting in a flame-reducing effect. The oxidizing flame is made by holding the tip of the blowpipe just inside the alcohol flame (as shown), and the extra oxygen entering the flame, through the pipe, has an oxidizing effect which causes a bluer, hotter flame to be produced. During blowpiping the cheeks are kept distended and act like bellows, as they supply a steady stream of air. All breathing is done through the nose. With a little practice a person soon becomes proficient.

It is then necessary to discover if the flames produced are of the desired type. This is best done, as follows, with a bead test. A loop roughly the diameter of a pencil lead is made in the end of a piece of platinum wire (or nichrome wire for manganese), and the alcohol lamp lit. The loop is heated in the lamp flame until red hot, then is dipped into the soda flux. A little of the flux will have adhered to the wire, and it is returned to the flame for reheating.

This is continued until a bead of flux fills the loop. The hot bead is then touched to powdered manganese dioxide (from the inside of a defunct flashlight battery—the black stuff), and is heated in the oxidizing flame. When the soda and manganese have fused together and the bead allowed to cool, the bead appears opaque greenish blue (robin's egg blue). If the bead is again heated, this time in the reducing flame, upon cooling it becomes colorless; back to the oxidizing flame it again becomes greenish blue; and so forth. Once a person can get the above results every time, they have a good handle on the type of flame they are producing.

The fluxes most commonly employed in bead tests are borax, sodium carbonate (or bicarbonate) and salt of phosphorus. Platinum wire is the preferred medium for all bead tests because it won't impart any color to any of the fluxes and won't melt in a blowpipe flame; though nichrome wire works adequately for manganese and cobalt compounds because they produce strong colors which mask any color from the nichrome wire. Remember, any wire should be cleaned thoroughly before another test is contemplated to prevent a false interpretation.

Often too much or too little powdered mineral is employed. If there is too much mineral, a very dark bead is produced. This is easily set right by heating the bead until fluid and, with a snap of the wrist, forcing most of it to fly from the loop. The remainder still on the wire is then diluted with more flux, and should give the correct color when reheated. If too little mineral is used, just add more powdered mineral. Below are listed the fluxes needed to produce the beads and the elements to impart the colors. All colors shown are for cold beads. Some of the elements and reactions have been noted previously; some, such as vanadium and titanium, not at all. However, since the vanadium bead color is similar to that of iron, and titanium to that of molybdenum, I would have been remiss in leaving them out. At the end of this section I've included further tests for vanadium and titanium.

Powdered element	Oxidizing flame	Reducing flame
Borax flux		
Iron (Fe)	Greenish	Pale green
Chromium (Cr)	Yellowish green	Green
Copper (Cu)	Blue	Reddish brown (opaque)
Nickel (Ni)	Brownish	Gray (opaque)
Manganese (Mn)	Reddish violet	Colorless
Uranium (U)	Yellow to brown	Pale green
Vanadium (V)	Greenish	Fine green
Molybdenum (Mo)	Colorless	Brown
Titanium (Ti)	Colorless	Brownish
Cobalt (Co)	Blue	Blue
Salt of phosphorus flux		
Tungsten (W)	Colorless	Fine blue
Uranium (U)	Greenish yellow	Fine green
Vanadium (V)	Yellowish	Fine green
Chromium (Cr)	Green	Green
Cobalt (Co)	Blue	Blue
Titanium (Ti)	Colorless	Pale violet
Soda flux		
Manganese (Mn)	Bluish green (opaque)	
Chromium (Cr)	Yellow (opaque)	

Vanadium minerals usually reveal themselves from those containing iron, by the evolution of chlorine gas and a cherry red color when strong hydrochloric acid is added (about 3 or 4 times as much acid as mineral) to a test tube containing the powdered mineral. For titanium, fuse with soda in the reducing flame on a charcoal block, dissolve in concentrated sulfuric acid in a test tube, pour (slowly) into another test tube having an equal quantity of water, then add a few drops of hydrogen peroxide. If titanium is present an amber yellow color is seen. Or, drop the fused mass into a test tube with hydrochloric acid, drop in a piece of metallic tin and heat; a pale violet color indicates titanium.

Minerals thought to contain sulfur, arsenic, antimony or selenium, must be roasted on charcoal with a blowpipe before doing any bead tests with platinum wire. If they aren't preroasted, these elements can combine with the platinum from the wire and cause it to become brittle, and therefore useless.

Employing reducing and oxidizing flames with charcoal or plaster of Paris blocks and a mineral fragment or powdered mineral and flux results in identifying reactions when the heat is applied. In the case of turquoise a fragment will jump off the block, other mineral fragments leave rings of color (coatings). The color of the coatings helps identify some mineral elements as they are actually the elements that have been released by the heating and have settled on the charcoal or plaster.

To use the blocks with the flames, scoop out a small hollow in the charcoal or plaster, roughly 1/4 inch (6 mm) in diameter, close to the end of the block and light the alcohol lamp. Place the mineral fragment, or some powdered mineral and flux, into the hollow, tilt the block, and direct the alcohol flame onto the assay with the blowpipe (as shown) to produce a reduced flame effect. After blowpiping, the deposited coatings are examined, the location of the coating in relation to the assay and the color should identify what mineral elements are present. The fused mass should also be checked for magnetism, or lack of it (see Iron on p.22).

It seems appropriate, at this point, to give a list of the more common coatings to be found after blowpiping, without flux, a mineral fragment on a charcoal block.

Close to assay	Away from assay	Element suggested
Dense white	Bluish	Antimony (Sb)
None	Whitish	Arsenic (As)
Dark yellow when hot, cooling to paler yellow	Bluish white	Lead (Pb)
Pale yellow when hot, white when cold with a reddish ring nearer mineral fragment	Bluish	Molybdenum (Mo)

Close to assay	Away from assay	Element suggested
Pale yellow when hot, white when cold	Faint white	Tin (Sb)
Canary yellow when hot, white when cold	Faint white	Zinc (Zn)

Cobalt Nitrate

Cobalt nitrate is desirable when testing for zinc, and occasionally aluminum. After a mineral fragment has been heated on charcoal, a drop of cobalt nitrate is added to the fragment or its coating. The fragment is then reheated, creating a reaction and a color is given off: blue for aluminum and green for zinc. Cobalt nitrate can be made if it can't be bought.

It is necessary to have both nitric acid and a cobalt compound to produce this chemical. The latter can often be found for sale in ceramics supplies stores, in the form of cobalt carbonate. The cobalt carbonate powder is added slowly to a container of dilute nitric acid, until all effervescence ceases and the liquid tests neutral with litmus paper. No heating is required during the process. This produces a fairly strong cobalt-nitrate solution; so, before using, it should be diluted with distilled water until it appears more like red wine vinegar in color. If the uncommon, natural mineral sphaerocobaltite is to be had, it can take the place of the processed cobalt carbonate. With either the manufactured or natural cobalt compounds, practice bead tests may be performed for the element.

Barium Chloride

Used to test for gypsum, this chemical is easy to produce, as long as the ingredients are obtainable. It is produced in a similar fashion to cobalt nitrate. A barium compound is required along with hydrochloric acid. I found barium carbonate in a ceramics supplies store. Muratic acid can be employed instead of the more expensive hydrochloric acid. The chemical compound is added slowly to the acid, without the need of heat, until all bubbling ceases. During the effervescence there will be a fairly unpleasant odor to contend with. The barium chloride is then ready for use. (Make only enough in a test tube for a few tests, because as with all solutions made with acid—the fewer poisonous things hanging around, the better.) If I'd been able to obtain some of the mineral witherite, a natural barium carbonate, I could have use that instead of the manufactured compound. Practice bead tests can be made with either the natural or manufactured barium compounds; practice flame tests can also be made.

Streak Plates

A mineral's color can greatly assist in determining what the mineral is. The color is obtained by rubbing the mineral onto a streak plate, to produce a streak of powder. The streak left by minerals can vary vastly. For instance, black hematite gives a red streak and brassy pyrite gives a greenish black streak.

The streak plate I'm familiar with is an unglazed tile, hexagonal in shape, 1 inch (25 mm) across the face, by 3/16-inch (5 mm) thick, with a hardness of 7 on Mohs' scale.

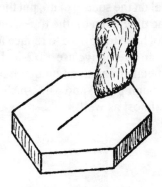

Streak plate (not to scale).

Always carry an eraser with the streak plate to remove the mineral powder before another streak is made. However, if a streak plate is unobtainable, there are temporary alternatives such as the unglazed back of a regular tile; the broken edge of a plate, cup or bowel; fine, light-colored sandpaper; a piece of fine, light-colored grinding wheel; a fragment of smooth concrete; a piece of opaque, massive quartz or quartzite; or a light-colored silicate pebble.

With a little unglazed tile as a streak plate, all minerals, up to a hardness of 7 on Mohs' scale of hardnesses, can be checked for the color of their streak: because the unglazed tile has a hardness of 7.

So don't believe those books that list streaks for corundum, at 9; topaz, at 8; or any minerals over 7 in hardness. It's just not possible with an unglazed tile.

The only way to figure out what the streak of a mineral more than 7 would look like, would be to take a small piece of the mineral and crush it to a fine powder.

See a list of streaks a prospector may find useful in the Appendix.

A Small Mineral Crusher

Several of the identifying tests require that the mineral be isolated from the surrounding rock and that the mineral be in powdered form. The easiest way to do this is to crush the rock.

A handy little pulverizer can be produced from a piece of 3/4-inch (19 mm) steel pipe about 1 inch (25 mm) long, a length of 5/8-inch (16 mm) diameter by 1 1/2-inch-long (38 mm) round steel rod, and a section of flat steel 3/8-inch (10 mm) thick by 2-inch (50 mm) square. If only 1/2-inch (13 mm) pipe is available, use a 3/8-inch (10 mm) round steel rod. To use, place the piece of mineral on the square plate, put the pipe over the sample and put the rod inside the pipe, then hit the top of the rod with a hammer. The hammer blows do not have to be hard to reduce most rock and mineral fragments to powder. As an alternative use a 1/2-inch or 3/4-inch (13 or 19 mm) pipe cap (a small metal cup with a female thread that is used to stop liquids from flowing through pipes) and a 1/2-inch or 3/4-inch (13 or 19 mm) bolt, they'll work almost as well.

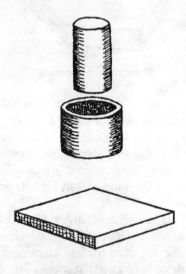

Small mineral crusher.

Aqua Regia

When a rock is encountered and is thought to contain gold, although it is invisible to the naked eye, this combination of acids will dissolve any gold therein.

Royal water, so called because of its capability to dissolve gold and other noble metals, is a combination of hydrochloric acid and nitric acid, full strength, in the ratio of 3 or 4 parts of the former to 1 part of the latter. The *aqua regia* is used with some of the powdered mineral, some tin, an alcohol lamp and a test tube to test for gold. (See section on gold on p.16).

Caution: All acids, especially at full strength, can prove lethal if used incorrectly and/or carelessly. After using, neutralize with bicarbonate of soda or washing soda in a plastic pail filled with water.

Mercury

Mercury, the liquid metal, has the ability to adhere to gold; therefore, processed gold objects can be identified as gold if any hallmarks have worn off, through the use of mercury.

Sources of mercury are few and far between. I know of only a few. At one time I worked with a man who was hard of hearing, and was able to get a steady supply of hearing aid batteries. To remove the quicksilver I simply crushed each battery with a pair of snips, over a shallow dish. Another source is from an old furnace thermostat; yet another source is old thermometers.

Common Identifying Acids

Most mineral testing requiring acids is done with acids in a diluted form. Diluted acids mean a lesser chance of a violent reaction, as there could be in the meeting of a strong acid and a chemical. Also it is cheaper to use the acids if they are diluted. The acids generally employed in mineral identification are: hydrochloric acid, nitric acid and sulfuric acid. These are usually used in diluted form as follows:

Acid	Ratio
hydrochloric	2 parts acid, 3 to 18 parts distilled water
nitric	2 parts acid, 3 parts distilled water
sulfuric	1 part acid 4 to 6 parts distilled water

Always pour the acid slowly into the distilled water; never the other way around. In the event full-strength acid is recommended for testing in a test tube, simply boil the diluted acid to evaporate some of the water. Hydrochloric acid is often more easily bought in a hardware store under the name of muratic acid. This impure form of hydrochloric acid is perfectly acceptable to test minerals.

Acetic acid (vinegar) can be used, full strength, to test some carbonates, such as trona.

Dropper bottles are required to hold and dispense acids and other liquid chemicals. It doesn't really matter whether they are glass or plastic. However, they should be well washed before adding testing chemicals.

Caution: Acids don't respect clothing or skin. Take care. Only employ them when absolutely necessary. Keep them locked away when not in use. Do not dispose of acids by way of the sewer system.

Flame Tests

Different elements give off different colors when burned. Sometimes the element in a mineral won't show its color, when burned, until it is in powdered form, while others do so readily when a chunk is held with tweezers in a flame. These tests are easy to perform and usually give the most satisfying and positive results.

There are two ways to conduct flame tests. The first is with a piece of an unknown mineral held in a pair of tweezers, dipped in acid (if necessary), and then placed into the side of an alcohol flame. The second method is with powdered mineral, acid or water, and a piece of iron wire or nichrome wire. The acid or water are required to help stick the powder to the wire. The list below states which acid should be used with certain elements.

Prior to beginning, the wire should be cleaned by dipping in hydrochloric acid several times, and burning it off each time in the alcohol lamp flame. The end of the wire is then moistened with the required liquid, and drawn through the powdered mineral. (Lenses from old spectacles make excellent receptacles for liquids and powders during flame tests.)

The wire with the adhering powder is placed on the outer edge at the side of the flame, and the resulting color, if any, will be seen mostly at the top of the flame. The color may be a strong showing or a brief flash. Sometimes the color of one element masks another. Sodium yellow is most often the guilty party. Following are listed the element, the acid (if necessary) and flame colors obtained. The iron wire should be thrown away after each test.

Element	Acid	Flame color
Lithium (Li)		Crimson
Strontium (Sr)	Hydrochloric	Crimson
Calcium (Ca)	Hydrochloric	Reddish yellow
Sodium (Na)		Yellow
Molybdenum (Mo)		Pale yellow-green
Barium (Ba)	Hydrochloric	Yellowish green
Boron (B)	Sulfuric	Yellowish green
Copper (Cu)		Emerald green

Zinc (Zn)		Blue-green
Phosphorus (P)	Sulfuric	Bluish green
Antimony (Sb)		Bluish green or light green
Bismuth (Bi)		Whitish green
Lead (Pb)		Whitish blue
Tellurium (Te)		Pale blue
Arsenic (As)		Light blue
Selenium (Se)		Darkish blue
Copper (Cu)	Hydrochloric	Azure blue
Potassium (K)		Violet

Note that copper is mentioned twice: with water it is green, with acid it is blue (copper chloride).

Chemicals and How Some Are Prepared

I've listed the chemicals I use most often during testing. Most mineral elements can be identified from the chemical reactions that occur when the chemicals come in contact with the elements. In cases where there may be some difficulty in obtaining certain chemicals, I have listed other chemicals which may be more easily found and work almost as well.

ALCOHOL—I've had great success with vodka (bought purely for medicinal purposes, I assure you) dissolving dimethylglyoxime. Used in nickel tests.

AMMONIUM HYDROXIDE—dilute 1 part acid to 2 parts of distilled water. Use household ammonia full strength. Do not employ sudsy ammonia. Used in copper, iron and nickel tests.

AMMONIUM MOLYBDATE—I've only mentioned a dry use for it; nevertheless, it can be prepared as follows to add to a test tube when testing for phosphorus. Mix 10 gm with 40 ml of distilled water and 8 ml of concentrated ammonia. Into this, pour a mixture of 40 ml of full-strength nitric acid and 60 ml distilled water. Stir slowly and constantly and then let stand for several days and filter before use. Used in phosphorus tests.

BARIUM CHLORIDE—used in testing for gypsum. If bought in powder form, add a little of it to a mixture of hydrochloric acid and possibly gypsum in a test tube, otherwise a few drops of barium chloride solution should be added to the test tube mixture.

COBALT NITRATE—in powder form, mix 7 gm with 100 mls of distilled water. Used in zinc and aluminum tests.

DIMETHYLGLYOXIME—dissolve 1 gm in 100 mls of alcohol, it does not dissolve in water. I've put just enough of the chemical to stay on the tip of a knife blade into a test tube and covered it with alcohol several hours prior to a test with some success. Used in nickel tests.

DRANO—I've listed this under its trade name because I'm not certain if it is pure sodium hydroxide, but it works just as well. Used in antimony tests.

HYDROGEN PEROXIDE—employ as bought, can be obtained from a drug store. Used in manganese and titanium tests.

POTASSIUM IODIDE—use dry mixed with sulfur; or combine 8 grams of the chemical with 100 mls of distilled water for test-tube testing of lead.

SODIUM CARBONATE (washing soda)—use dry. Sodium bicarbonate (baking soda) can be substituted for most tests, except those involving mercury. Used as a flux for bead testing and also used as a flux on charcoal.

SODIUM CHLORIDE—employ dry. Pickling salt, not iodized, can also be used in silver tests.

SULFUR—mixed 1 to 1 with potassium iodide used as a flux for bismuth and molydenum, also lead.

TURMERIC— used dampened in tests for sodium, potassium, barium, calcium and strontium.

I discovered a source of sulfur (for mixing with potassium iodide), without really looking for it, while visiting a Fraser River bar on the north side of the river just west of Hope, B.C. The sulfur chunks were scattered along the train tracks, having fallen from a train on the way to Vancouver.

The chemicals mentioned are simple to mix, if one knows that 5 milliliters (mls) = 1 teaspoon and 1 gram (gm) = 1/30 of an ounce.

The tiny spoon that one gets when purchasing a cup of coffee at McDonald's can come in handy for dispensing small amounts of chemicals.

Caution: Employ care when using any chemicals. Always wear safety glasses, especially when using chemicals with acids.

Turmeric Paper

There are more than 100 elements in existence. If, with a little piece of paper, a person can identify 5 of the elements, then that paper is worth producing. On the other hand, if a negative result is obtained, that leaves about 95 other alternatives. As previously stated, turmeric paper is employed as a common test for barium, calcium, potassium, sodium and strontium, see that section of the book for further testing instructions (see p.37). These elements give an alkaline reaction on the treated paper.

This testing paper is cheap to make. Purchase a small package of the spice, and some blotting paper (the paper should be available at a stationary store if it is still to be had in this age of ballpoint pens). In the event blotting paper is unavailable, use thick paper towel. Mix a strong solution of turmeric powder and water, so that it is almost a paste, and pour into a shallow bowl. Soak pieces of the blotting paper (or paper towel) in the solution, then hang up to dry. When dry, cut the paper into 1/2-inch (13 mm) squares, and put them into a watertight container until required. In the event a person doesn't wish to make the above paper, the spice can be used in the following way. Into the concave side of a watch glass or a lens from an old pair of spectacles, put a sprinkling of turmeric, dampen with water and place the roasted mineral on top; then wait for the red stain to appear.

Taste Testing

Another test to consider is the one undertaken with the tongue; especially if the mineral appears to be the deposit of an evaporated solution. Only a tiny particle should be tasted, then the mouth thoroughly rinsed. The reason being, some minerals, such as chalcanthite, are poisonous and may make a person ill. The following is a list of well-known minerals and how they taste.

Mineral	Taste
Borax (Borate)	sweetish, astringent
Trona (Carbonate)	alkaline (soda)
Chalcanthite (Sulfate)	metallic, sweetish
Copiapite (Sulfate)	metallic
Epsomite (Sulfate)	bitter
Glauberite (Sulfate)	slightly bitter, salty
Polyhalite (Sulfate)	bitter
Thenardite (Sulfate)	salty
Carnallite (Ilalide)	bitter, salty
Halite (Halide)	salty
Sylvite (Halide)	salty, but bitter
Sal ammoniac (Halide)	bitter
Niter (Nitrate)	a cooling feeling
Soda niter (Nitrate)	a cooling feeling
Magnesite (Carbonate)	no distinguishing taste; but the tongue will adhere to the mineral surface.

Comments:

My first conscious taste test occurred when I was 4 or 5 years old, at school, and was given a scratchy steel pen and ink for the first time. Of course my foremost thought was purely scientific, and I dipped my finger into the ink well to taste it. Little did I know that I would recognize copiapite years later by the same metallic flavor. Another time I was about 13 years of age, several miles from home, and hiking across a field through a flock of sheep. There on the ground in front of me reclined a beautiful glassy rock, colored blue-gray, white and clear in irregular patches and bands. In a region of chalk, sand, clay and flint, it stood out like a snowman in the Sahara. I decided, after much deliberation, to taste it, and found it to be halite (rock salt)—and I had licked where about 50 sheep had also been licking!

Testing in the Field

With the limited amount of tools that one can carry on a field trip, it's still possible, with a few simple tests, to check whether a mineral specimen is worth carrying home for those tests of a more complex nature.

Although a rock hammer is especially designed for removing, by force, interesting specimens, if possible carry a small 3 or 4 pound sledge hammer and a couple of chisels. They make collecting so much easier and are worth the added weight in the backpack. Don't forget safety glasses, never hammer at rocks without them on.

The eyes are the first determining tools to use. But don't jump to any hasty conclusions—they can lead to disappointments. If you're hoping to find gold, pyrite looks mighty attractive. So check the color of the specimen against the streak produced when it's rubbed across a streak plate. Some minerals instantly identify themselves in this way. Native gold has a gold streak; whereas brassy-looking pyrite has a greenish black streak. Hematite comes in a variety of colors, but the streak is always some shade of red or reddish brown. Molybdenite, graphite and pyrolusite leave a dark mark if rubbed on paper. Use a page from your notebook as a testing tool. With galena, the color of the mineral is similar to the streak, as is cinnabar. But these are exceptions to the general rule of rock or mineral color being more often different from the streak. But before we leave those specimens easily identified this way, don't always look on pyrite as fool's gold. Remember, it's occasionally found associated with gold or chalcopyrite.

Stains and coatings on rocks with minute particles of economic minerals disseminated through them can often indicate what is nearby. Sometimes they are the tips of valuable icebergs, so to speak. A pretty, eye-catching green stain, in some instances close to emerald green, can indicate copper. A rusty coating indicates iron, but there is always the possibility of something interesting beneath it. A light green coating or crust that could be mistaken for moss at a glance can indicate the mineral annerbergite and nickel. Erythrite is a secondary mineral having cobalt and nickel in the compound and has earthy crusts or coatings from pinkish blue to deep reddish purple in color—known as cobalt bloom. The former color indicates some nickel present; the latter shows when cobalt dominates. Uranophane, a soft, canary yellow, crusty mineral found at or near the surface of uranium deposits is known as uranium stain.

A prospector will occasionally come across crystals. If they are glassy looking there is always the question: are they diamonds? Probably not. To me, quartz crystals appear more like diamonds than rough diamonds do.

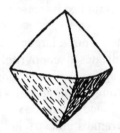  

Left to Right: Diamond crystal; quartz crystal; corundum crystal.

Diamond crystal: found as octohedrons with curved faces, often misshapen.
Corundum crystal: if held between the finger and thumb, top and bottom, and turned,
    6 major faces can be counted, whereas the diamond crystal would show 4 edges.
Quartz crystal: also would show 6 major faces, but the points are generally much
    sharper than the more often chunky corundum crystal.

After visually inspecting a specimen, the next tests should be with a pocket knife. Test if the specimen is softer than the knife blade by scraping or attempting to cut it. Silver, copper, lead and mercury minerals seldom exceed 3 on Mohs' scale, and are easily cut or powdered by the blade. The blade is about 5.5 on the same scale. The blade should also be magnetized, by rubbing it repeatedly with a strong bar magnet in one direction only, to identify some of the magnetic minerals that could be attracted to it, e.g., magnetite, nickel-iron mixtures, pyrrhotite and platinum-iron mixtures.

Heft. If the specimen feels far heavier than it should for its size when judged for weight in the palm of one's hand, it could contain minerals with the following elements: platinum, mercury, uranium, gold, lead or tin. Judge it for weight with a piece of common rock, of similar size, held in the other hand. Before leaving the subject of heft, it should be mentioned that few light-colored, glassy minerals can be identified in this way, being mostly at the lower end of the scale. Barite is an exception, at about 4.5 specific gravity. (It is well worth learning to identify this mineral because it can be found with lead, silver and antimony sulfides.)

Attempt to scratch the specimen with a thumb nail. Talc (the main ingredient in talcum powder) and gypsum are easily marked and can be identified this way. Soapstone is an impure form of talc; slightly harder, but still scratchable with a thumb nail. It is an excellent find. There are many soapstone carvers who could be possible customers.

Rub the specimen with your thumb. If it feels greasy it could indicate molybdenite, soapstone or serpentine. The latter is also a carving material. Serpentine, which ranges from whitish, green and red, to black with a whitish streak, can usually be scratched with a knife blade; it is occasionally found near jade (nephrite) deposits. I've found several outcrops of serpentine—as yet no jade. When barite is rubbed it sometimes gives off an unpleasant smell.

If the specimen has been removed by a hammer, from a larger rock, smell it directly after the blow. A garliclike odor indicates arsenopyrite. If there's no noticeable odor, breath on it and smell again. An earthy odor (quite strong) indicates orthoclase feldspar; interesting, but not usually of economic importance. However if a large deposit is found, it may be worth a second look because feldspars are used in the ceramics industry in the making of glazes.

Taste testing can identify some minerals, most of which are only valuable in large deposits. Chalcanthite, the sky blue copper mineral, has a sweetish, metallic taste. If it is found it could indicate worthwhile nearby deposits of copper. But always make notes of the locations of any minerals identified by taste testing, one never knows what they could lead to. Rinse the mouth thoroughly after all taste tests.

The specimens should also be tested with dilute hydrochloric acid. I always carry a small dropper bottle of such (1 part acid to 9 parts distilled water) on field trips. It rides inside a larger plastic container with a tight-fitting lid, padded with paper towel, to ensure it doesn't leak and eat holes in my backpack. I employ it to identify carbonate minerals, such as calcite, by dropping a little of it on to a specimen. When treated in this way, some carbonates readily bubble (effervesce) and give off carbon dioxide. Others react similarly after powdering, placing into a test tube with the dilute acid, and heating over an alcohol lamp. Learn to recognize the carbonates—some yield copper, zinc, lead, etc.

A few words about acids...though they shouldn't be feared, acids must be treated with respect. A nonchalant approach to using them, could end up with a fast trip to the emergency ward of a hospital. Only use diluted acids unless otherwise stated. They are all that is usually required to obtain a desired result; besides they are safer and cheaper. Keep acids out of reach of children. This also holds true for chemicals employed in testing, and the solutions that are left after tests have been completed. Conduct all tests in well-ventilated areas.

It's here I should mention something about fracture and cleavage (no,

I'm not talking about Madonna). Fracture is the uneven breakage of a mineral or rock. Cleavage is the propensity to break along certain lines. In larger mineral specimens, both are easily seen and could provide a means of positive identification. But I don't think they would be of much use to a weekend prospector unfamiliar with them, and could lead to confusion. On field trips most specimens found are often small mineral particles in large rocks, with the fractures and cleavages difficult to determine. There are, however, a couple of exceptions to this. See nephrite jade and chert in the lapidary section on p.45, 53.

The most important tools to take when prospecting I've left to the last. They are a notebook and pencil. They are used to record the location of a find in case further exploration is warranted. Never trust your memory in this regard. Record it now; don't leave it until later. Use a compass to determine north and pace off the find from easily seen landmarks. Be precise. If the find is too obvious, hide it with rocks and branches so there is less chance of someone else seeing it before a decision is reached whether to stake a claim or not.

Following is a basic list of equipment to take on a field trip. One should take along a rock hammer, a small sledge hammer, chisels and safety glasses. One should also pack a gold pan, a knife, hydrochloric acid, a note book and pencil, a magnet, a streak plate and an eraser, a set of hardness points and tungsten carbide. One should also have small containers, such as pill bottles, for the gold panned and plastic bags in which to put samples. This equipment should all fit into a backpack. For those who wish to take more than the basics here are a few more items that won't add too much weight to the pack: a blowpipe, candle, charcoal block, tweezers, some washing or baking soda, some platinum wire, a test tube, some water and dilute hydrochloric acid, and some turmeric paper. Make certain all the equipment is stored in a safe manner, you don't want any broken glass or hydrochloric acid making holes in your backpack. And don't forget to take along this book!

As it's more fun working with specimens you've found, go on collecting trips, as many as possible. If buying specimens, do so from a reputable establishment. When passing through small communities on holiday, take the time to visit any museums therein. Often rocks and minerals found locally are on display. If they are of interest, stay a few days and try to add to your collection. Happy prospecting!

Streak Test Appendix

STREAK	MINERAL	ELEMENT(S)
Black	Ilmenite	Titanium
Black	Magnetite	Iron
Black	Pyrite	Iron
Black	Pyrolusite	Manganese
Brownish black to black	Ferberite	Tungsten
Brownish black to black	Wolframite	Tungsten
Shiny brownish black	Psilomelane	Manganese
Dark brown, almost black	Chromite	Chromium
Pale brownish black	Niccolite	Nickel
Gray, brown to almost black	Uraninite (pitchblende)	Uranium
Shiny dark gray to black	Argentite	Silver
Dark gray to black	Arsenopyrite	Arsenic
Grayish black	Cobaltite	Cobalt
Grayish black	Native silver (tarnished)	Silver
Grayish black	Pyrrhotite	Iron
Grayish black to black	Smaltite	Cobalt
Lead gray to black	Covellite	Copper
Light grayish black	Bornite	Copper
Greenish black	Chalcopyrite	Copper
Greenish black	Millerite	Nickel
Darkish lead gray	Chalcocite	Copper
Steel gray to lead gray	Stibnite	Antimony
Lead gray	Clausthalite	Selenium & lead
Lead gray	Galena	Lead
Steel gray	Bismuthinite	Bismuth
Grayish	Cassiterite	Tin
Blue gray	Molybdenite	Molybdenum
Blue (paler than mineral)	Azurite	Copper
Brownish	Cassiterite	Tin

Reddish brown	Hematite	Iron
Brownish red	Ilmenite	Titanium
Yellow-brown, brownish	Limonite-geothite	Iron
Pale brown, bronze	Pentlandite	Iron & nickel
Pale brown	Rutile	Titanium
Pale brown	Sphalerite	Zinc
Scarlet	Cinnabar	Mercury
Brilliant red	Pyrargyrite	Silver
Orange-red to bright red	Realgar	Arsenic
Cherry red	Hematite	Iron
Reddish purple	Proustite	Silver
Brick red	Greenockite	Cadmium
Shiny gold	Native gold	Gold
Shiny copper	Native copper	Copper
Orange-yellow	Greenockite	Cadmium
Lemon yellow (paler than mineral)	Orpiment	Arsenic
Yellow	Limonite-geothite	Iron
Yellow	Sphalerite	Zinc
Yellowish	Vanadinite	Vanadium
Pale green (paler than mineral)	Malachite	Copper
Shiny silver white	Native bismuth	Bismuth
Silver white	Native silver	Silver
Tin white	Native antimony	Antimony
Tin white	Native tellurium	Tellurium
Off white	Cassiterite	Tin
White	Amblygonite	Lithium & phosphorus
White	Apatite	Phosphorus
White	Aragonite	Calcium
White	Barite	Barium
White	Boracite	Boron
White	Borax	Boron
White	Calcite	Calcium
White	Carnallite	Potassium

White	Celestite	Strontium
White	Colemanite	Boron
White	Copiapite	Iron
White	Dolomite	Calcium & magnesium
White	Epsomite	Magnesium
White	Fluorite	Fluorine
White	Glauberite	Sodium & calcium
White	Gypsum	Calcium
White	Halite (common salt)	Sodium & chlorine
White	Kernite	Boron
White	Lepidolite	Lithium & potassium
White	Magnesite	Magnesium
White	Scheelite	Tungsten
White	Siderite	Iron
White	Smithsonite	Zinc
White	Soda niter	Nitrogen
White	Sphalerite	Zinc
White	Titanite	Titanium
White	Spodumene	Lithium
White	Strontianite	Strontium
White	Sylvite	Potassium
White	Thenardite	Sodium
White	Trona	Sodium
White	Ulexite	Boron
White	Vanadinite	Vanadium
White	Witherite	Barium
White	Wulfenite	Lead & molybdenum
Uncolored to white	Niter	Nitrogen
Uncolored	Anglesite	Lead
Uncolored	Cerussite	Lead
Uncolored	Orthoclase feldspar	Potassium & aluminum
Uncolored	Petalite	Lithium

Lapidary Rocks and Minerals Index

Field Testing Index

General Index